W9-ARA-187

Date: 6/8/15

J 912 GAN
Ganeri, Anita,
Around the world : a colorful
atlas for kids /

PALM BEACH COUNTY
LIBRARY SYSTEM
3650 Summit Boulevard
West Palm Beach, FL 33406-4198

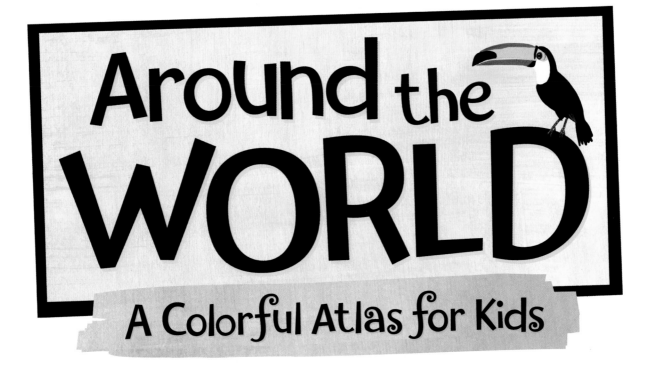

Around the WORLD

A Colorful Atlas for Kids

ILLUSTRATED BY CHRISTOPHER CORR
WRITTEN BY ANITA GANERI

ALBERT WHITMAN & COMPANY
CHICAGO, ILLINOIS

Contents

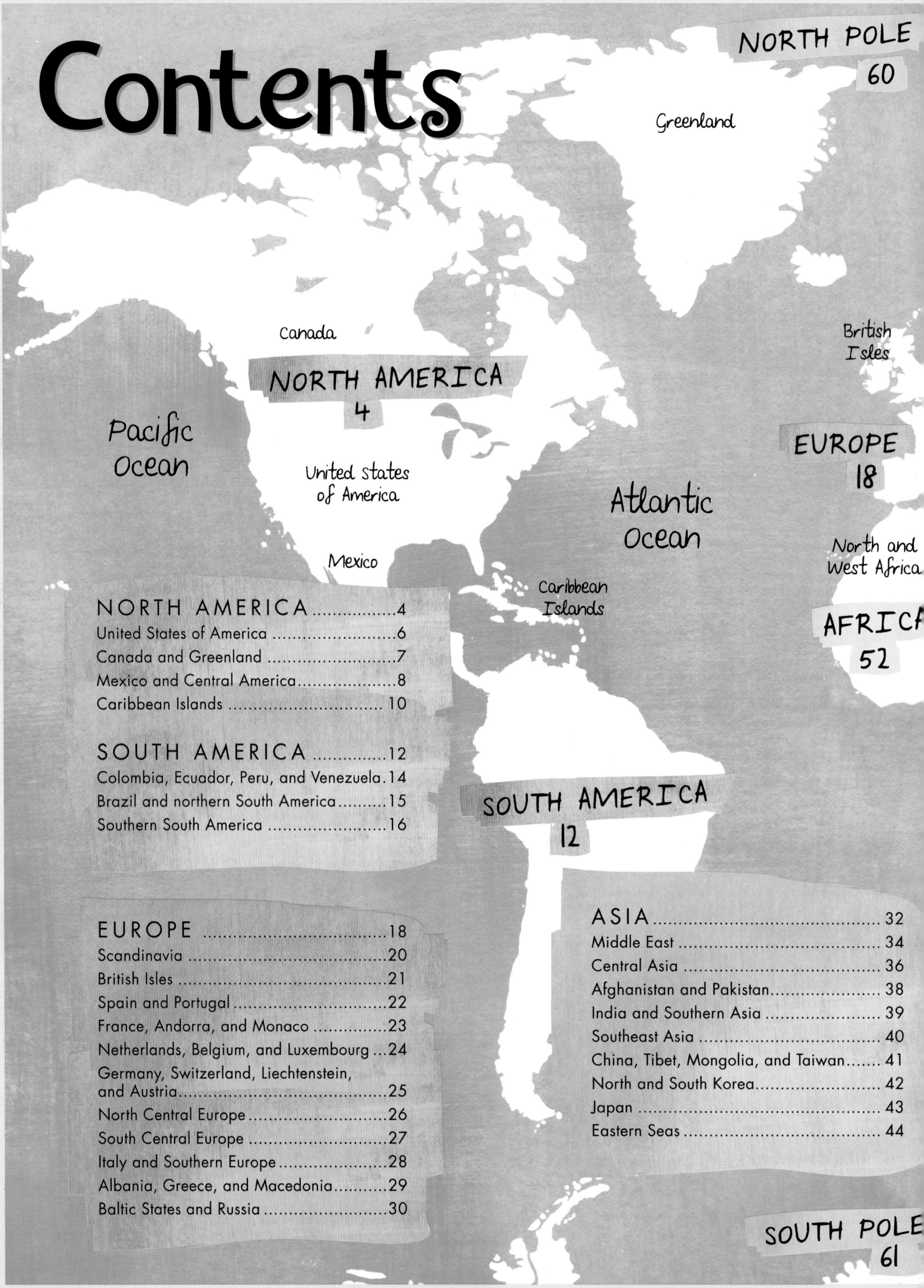

NORTH POLE
60

Greenland

Canada

NORTH AMERICA
4

Pacific
Ocean

United states
of America

Mexico

British
Isles

EUROPE
18

North and
West Africa

Atlantic
Ocean

Caribbean
Islands

AFRICA
52

SOUTH AMERICA
12

SOUTH POLE
61

Arctic
Ocean

Russia

Scandinavia

Baltic
states

ASIA
32

central
Europe

central Asia

Middle
East

Southern
Asia

China

Japan

Pacific
Ocean

Southeast
Asia

East
Africa

central
Africa

Indian
Ocean

Pacific
Islands

Southern
Africa

Australia

OCEANIA
46

New
Zealand

Southern Ocean

Antarctica

North America

North America is the third largest continent on Earth. It is made up of Canada, the United States of America (USA), Mexico, the islands of the Caribbean, the seven countries of Central America, and Greenland, the world's largest island. Canada and the USA are the biggest countries by far. North America has snowcapped mountains, baking deserts, huge lakes, and long rivers. It is also famous for its big, bustling cities, such as New York City and Mexico City.

Arctic Ocean

ALASKA (USA)

Pacific Ocean

Rocky Mountains

Hawaii (USA)

GREENLAND

Hudson
Bay

CANADA

UNITED STATES
OF AMERICA

Appalachian Mountains

Atlantic Ocean

Gulf of
Mexico

MEXICO

BAHAMAS

VIRGIN
ISLANDS
PUERTO
RICO
ANTIGUA & BARBUDA

ST. KITTS &
NEVIS

DOMINICAN
REPUBLIC

DOMINICA

CUBA

HAITI

ST. LUCIA

BARBADOS

JAMAICA

ST. VINCENT &
THE GRENADINES

GRENADA

TRINIDAD
& TOBAGO

Caribbean Sea

BELIZE

GUATEMALA

HONDURAS

EL
SALVADOR

NICARAGUA

COSTA
RICA

PANAMA

United States of America

ALASKA

Humpback whale

Brown bear

Anchorage

CANADA

Pacific Ocean

Bald eagle

CANADA

Statue of Liberty
This huge statue is made from copper and stands in New York Harbor. It is as tall as 25 adults. People can climb right up into the crown.

Moose

Native American

Mt. Rushmore

Rocky Mountains

Niagara Falls

Chicago

Mayflower

New York city

Washington DC

Buffalo

Golden Gate Bridge

Mountain lion

HOLLYWOOD

Los Angeles

UNITED STATES OF AMERICA

Baseball

Kentucky Derby

Appalachian Mountains

Wright Brothers' plane

Atlantic Ocean

Grand Canyon
The Grand Canyon is a giant gash in Earth's surface. It was carved by water millions of years ago. It is about 1 mile deep.

Saguaro cacti

Armadillo

Jazz music

MEXICO

Gulf of Mexico

Manatee

CUBA

Cowboys
Cowboys herd cows and other animals. They gallop after the cows on horseback and catch them by throwing long ropes called lassos.

Pacific Ocean

HAWAII

Honolulu

Volcano

United states of America

How many faces are on Mt. Rushmore?

The United States of America (USA) is a huge country made up of 50 states. Most of the states are joined together except for Alaska and Hawaii. Alaska is in the far north next to Canada. Hawaii, a group of islands in the Pacific Ocean, was formed by volcanoes.

More than 313 million people live in the USA. It is one of the richest and most powerful countries on Earth. Many people live in big, modern cities. The city of Los Angeles is famous for being the home of Hollywood, where many movie stars live.

Answer: Four

Canada and Greenland

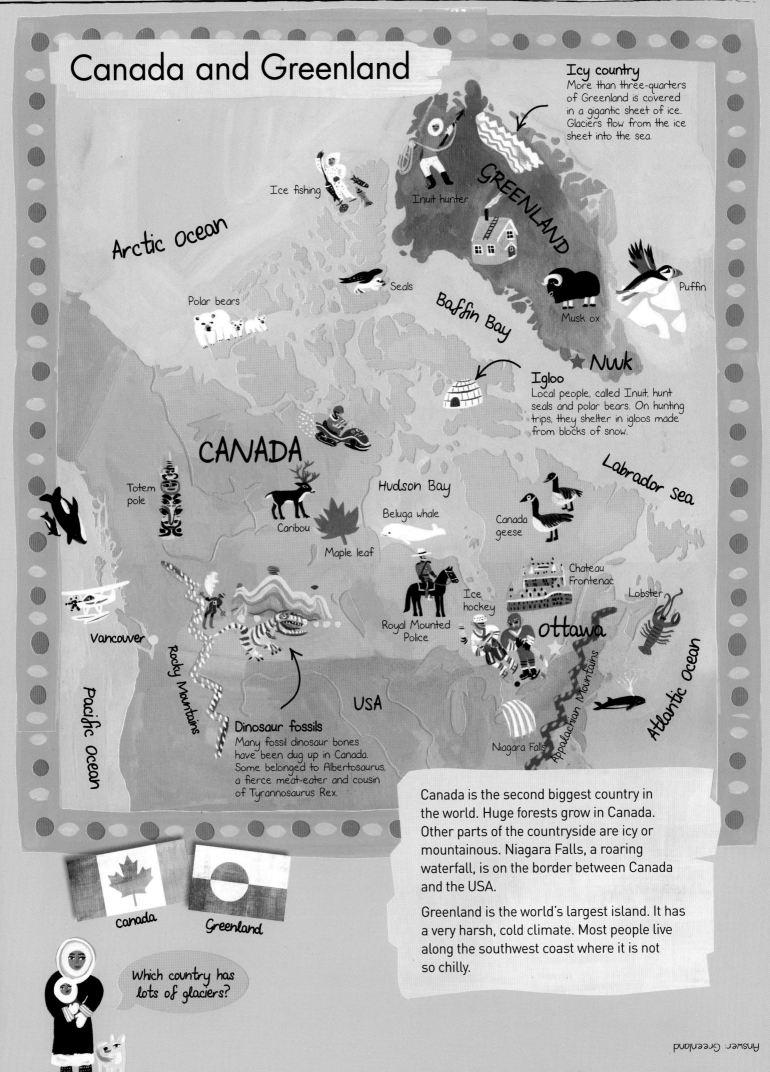

Icy country
More than three-quarters of Greenland is covered in a gigantic sheet of ice. Glaciers flow from the ice sheet into the sea.

Ice fishing

GREENLAND

Inuit hunter

Arctic Ocean

Seals

Baffin Bay

Polar bears

Puffin

Musk ox

Nuuk

Igloo
Local people, called Inuit, hunt seals and polar bears. On hunting trips, they shelter in igloos made from blocks of snow.

CANADA

Labrador sea

Totem pole

Hudson Bay

Beluga whale

Canada geese

Caribou

Maple leaf

Chateau Frontenac

Lobster

Ice hockey

Royal Mounted Police

Vancouver

Ottawa

Rocky Mountains

Appalachian Mountains

Pacific Ocean

Atlantic Ocean

USA

Dinosaur fossils
Many fossil dinosaur bones have been dug up in Canada. Some belonged to Albertosaurus, a fierce meat-eater and cousin of Tyrannosaurus Rex.

Niagara Falls

Canada is the second biggest country in the world. Huge forests grow in Canada. Other parts of the countryside are icy or mountainous. Niagara Falls, a roaring waterfall, is on the border between Canada and the USA.

Greenland is the world's largest island. It has a very harsh, cold climate. Most people live along the southwest coast where it is not so chilly.

canada

Greenland

Which country has lots of glaciers?

Answer: Greenland

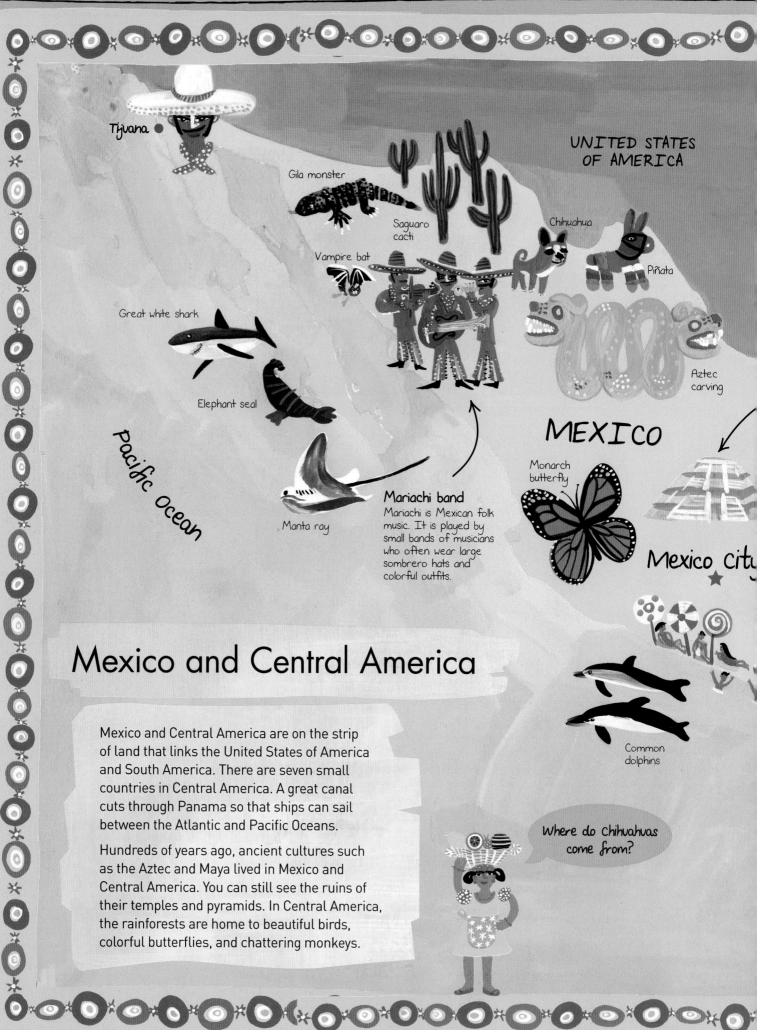

Tijuana

Gila monster

Saguaro cacti

Vampire bat

Great white shark

Elephant seal

UNITED STATES OF AMERICA

Chihuahua

Piñata

Aztec carving

MEXICO

Monarch butterfly

Pacific Ocean

Manta ray

Mariachi band
Mariachi is Mexican folk music. It is played by small bands of musicians who often wear large sombrero hats and colorful outfits.

Mexico city

Common dolphins

Mexico and Central America

Mexico and Central America are on the strip of land that links the United States of America and South America. There are seven small countries in Central America. A great canal cuts through Panama so that ships can sail between the Atlantic and Pacific Oceans.

Hundreds of years ago, ancient cultures such as the Aztec and Maya lived in Mexico and Central America. You can still see the ruins of their temples and pyramids. In Central America, the rainforests are home to beautiful birds, colorful butterflies, and chattering monkeys.

Where do Chihuahuas come from?

Answer: Mexico

Mexico

Guatemala

Belize

El salvador

Honduras

Nicaragua

Costa Rica

Panama

Leatherback turtle

Gulf of Mexico

Pyramid of the Sun
Soaring 20 stories above the ground, the Pyramid of the Sun was built around 2,000 years ago. At the top was a temple to the Aztec gods.

Lobster

Chichen Itza pyramid

Whale shark

Ancient Olmec stone carving

Jaguar

Tikal pyramid

BELIZE

Belmopan

Honduran white bat

GUATEMALA   Bananas

HONDURAS

Guatemala city

Tegucigalpa

Three-toed sloth

EL SALVADOR

san salvador

Managua   NICARAGUA

Harpy eagle

Resplendent quetzal
The quetzal is a gorgeous green-and-red bird from Central America. The money used in Guatemala is called the quetzal in its honor.

COSTA RICA   Hummingbird

san José

Morpho butterfly

Howler monkey

PANAMA   Panama city

BAHAMAS

CUBA

JAMAICA

Caribbean Sea

Atlantic Ocean

COLOMBIA

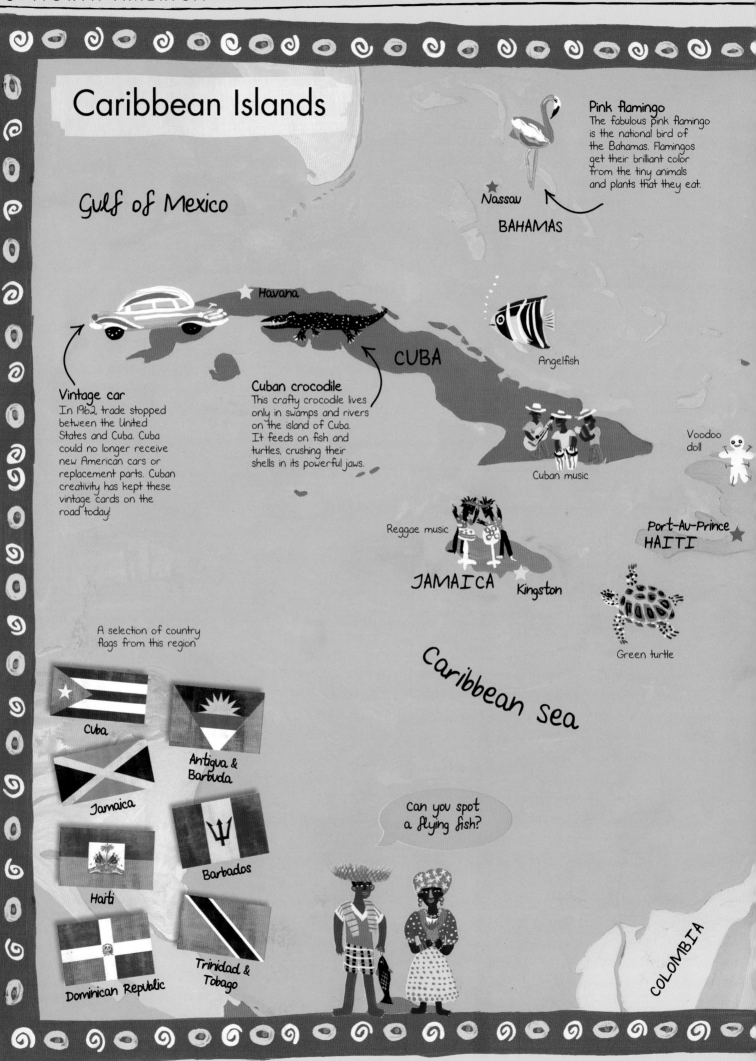

Caribbean Islands

Gulf of Mexico

Pink flamingo
The fabulous pink flamingo is the national bird of the Bahamas. Flamingos get their brilliant color from the tiny animals and plants that they eat.

★ Nassau
BAHAMAS

★ Havana

CUBA

Angelfish

Vintage car
In 1962, trade stopped between the United States and Cuba. Cuba could no longer receive new American cars or replacement parts. Cuban creativity has kept these vintage cars on the road today!

Cuban crocodile
This crafty crocodile lives only in swamps and rivers on the island of Cuba. It feeds on fish and turtles, crushing their shells in its powerful jaws.

Cuban music

Voodoo doll

Reggae music

Port-Au-Prince
HAITI

JAMAICA   Kingston

Green turtle

A selection of country flags from this region

Caribbean Sea

Cuba

Antigua & Barbuda

Jamaica

Barbados

Haiti

Can you spot a flying fish?

Dominican Republic

Trinidad & Tobago

COLOMBIA

Pirate ship
Hundreds of years ago, pirate ships prowled the Caribbean Sea on the lookout for treasure. On board were pirates, such as Blackbeard, who was famous for his fearsome looks.

To the east of Central America, hundreds of islands lie in the Caribbean Sea. The islands are known as the West Indies. Most of the large islands are also countries, including Jamaica, Barbados, Cuba, and Trinidad and Tobago.

Each year, millions of tourists visit the islands to enjoy the sunny weather and sandy beaches. They swim in the warm sea and snorkel over the colorful coral reefs. But the islands can also be hit by fierce storms, called hurricanes, which bring howling winds and pouring rain.

Atlantic Ocean

Palm tree

Frigate bird

Scuba diver

DOMINICAN REPUBLIC

Solenodon

VIRGIN ISLANDS

Mango

Mongoose

San Juan

Santo Domingo

PUERTO RICO

ST. KITTS & NEVIS

Basseterre

ANTIGUA & BARBUDA

St. John's

Sailboat

Fishing boat

DOMINICA

Roseau

Sperm whale

Leatherback turtle

Castries

ST. LUCIA

Cricket player

ST. VINCENT & THE GRENADINES

Kingstown

Bridgetown

Bananas

BARBADOS

St. George's

GRENADA

Flying fish

Manta ray

Spices

Port-of-spain

Anaconda

VENEZUELA

TRINIDAD & TOBAGO

South America

The fourth largest continent, South America is home to almost 400 million people. Its countries include Brazil, Argentina, and Peru. South America has some of the most spectacular scenery on Earth. The towering Andes mountains run all the way down the west side of the continent. To the east of the Andes is the Amazon Rainforest, the world's biggest rainforest.

FRENCH GUIANA

SURINAME

GUYANA

VENEZUELA

COLOMBIA

ECUADOR

PERU

Andes M

Galápagos Islands

BRAZIL

PARAGUAY

URUGUAY

BOLIVIA

ARGENTINA

CHILE

Andes Mountains

Atlantic Ocean

Pacific Ocean

Colombia, Ecuador, Peru, and Venezuela

Dancing devils
Dressed in bloodred clothes and wearing devil masks, people dance through the streets to celebrate the festival of Corpus Christi in Venezuela.

★ Caracas

Catatumbo lightning
Frequent powerful flashes of lightning occur over Lake Maracaibo 140 to 160 nights a year as many as 10 hours per day.

Poison-arrow frog

PANAMA

Golden Mask
This mask from Colombia was made from a sheet of gold about 2,000 years ago. It was probably placed over a deceased person's face before he was buried.

VENEZUELA

Angel Falls

Bushmaster snake

Bogotá ★

Heliconia

BRAZIL

Andean condor

Quito ★

COLOMBIA

Playing panpipes

ECUADOR

Amazon River

Machu Picchu
High in the Andes in Peru are the ruins of the ancient city of Machu Picchu. It was built by the Inca about 550 years ago, then mysteriously abandoned.

PERU

Llamas

Paddington Bear

The countries of Colombia, Ecuador, Peru, and Venezuela are at the north end of the Andes mountains. The mighty Amazon River begins high up in the mountains in Peru. The river flows an awesome 4,000 miles across the continent.

Venezuela is a country that has rich oil supplies. It also has the famous Angel Falls, the world's highest waterfall, which plunges 3,212 feet off a steep cliff. Off the coast of Ecuador lie the Galápagos Islands. They are home to some amazing animals, including giant tortoises and marine iguanas, that are not found anywhere else on Earth.

Lima ★

Andes Mountains

Sardines

Can you find the flag of Ecuador?

BOLIVIA

Reed boat

Lake Titicaca

Ecuador　　Peru　　Venezuela　　Colombia

VENEZUELA

COLOMBIA

Cock-of-the-rock bird

Leatherback turtle

Georgetown

Paramaribo

GUYANA

SURINAME

FRENCH GUIANA

Cayenne

Medicine man
A shaman is a wise man who is skilled in using rainforest plants as medicines. He passes on his knowledge to others in his tribe.

Amazon River dolphin

Crocodiles

Amazon River

Amazon Rainforest
The Amazon Rainforest covers an area about the size of Australia. More kinds of animals live here than anywhere else in the world.

BRAZIL

Indigenous Kayapo

PERU

Poisonous Coral snake

Carnival!
Every year in February or March it is carnival time in Rio de Janeiro. There are street parades with floats and dancers dressed in spectacular costumes.

BOLIVIA

Brasilia

Christ the Redeemer statue

Rio de Janeiro

Iguaçu Falls

Samba music

Brazil and northern South America

Brazil is the largest country in South America and covers almost half of the continent. The mighty Amazon River flows through Brazil on its way to the sea. On its banks grows the Amazon Rainforest, home to millions of animals and plants and local peoples.

Guyana and Suriname are two of the smallest countries in South America. Only about 750,000 people live in Guyana, mostly along the coast. Suriname used to be ruled by the Netherlands. French Guiana is still governed by France.

Georgetown is the capital of which country?

Guyana

Brazil

Suriname

Answer: Guyana

BRAZIL

Iguaçu Falls

Gaucho

Montevideo

Armadillo

URUGUAY

Streetcar

Folk costume
Many people in Bolivia still wear traditional clothes including striped ponchos, shawls, and hats.

Cattle

Parana River

Asunción

PARAGUAY

Spectacled bear

La Paz

Buenos Aires

BOLIVIA

Football
Soccer is known as football around the world.

ARGENTINA

Rhea

Giant bromeliad

Andes Mountains

Atacama Desert

CHILE

Andes Mountains

Santiago

PERU

Dolphins

Monkey puzzle tree
The odd-looking monkey puzzle tree grows in the mountains in Chile. It can grow 130 feet tall-that's almost as tall as eight giraffes.

Answer: Chile

Southern South America

The southern part of South America has a very varied landscape. Chile is a long, thin country that stretches along the west coast in between the sea and the Andes mountains. The Atacama Desert in the north is the driest place on Earth.

The pampas in Argentina and Uruguay are huge grassy plains used for growing crops and grazing cattle. At the southern tip of the region are the islands of Tierra del Fuego. They are wild and windswept with gigantic glaciers flowing from the mountains into the sea.

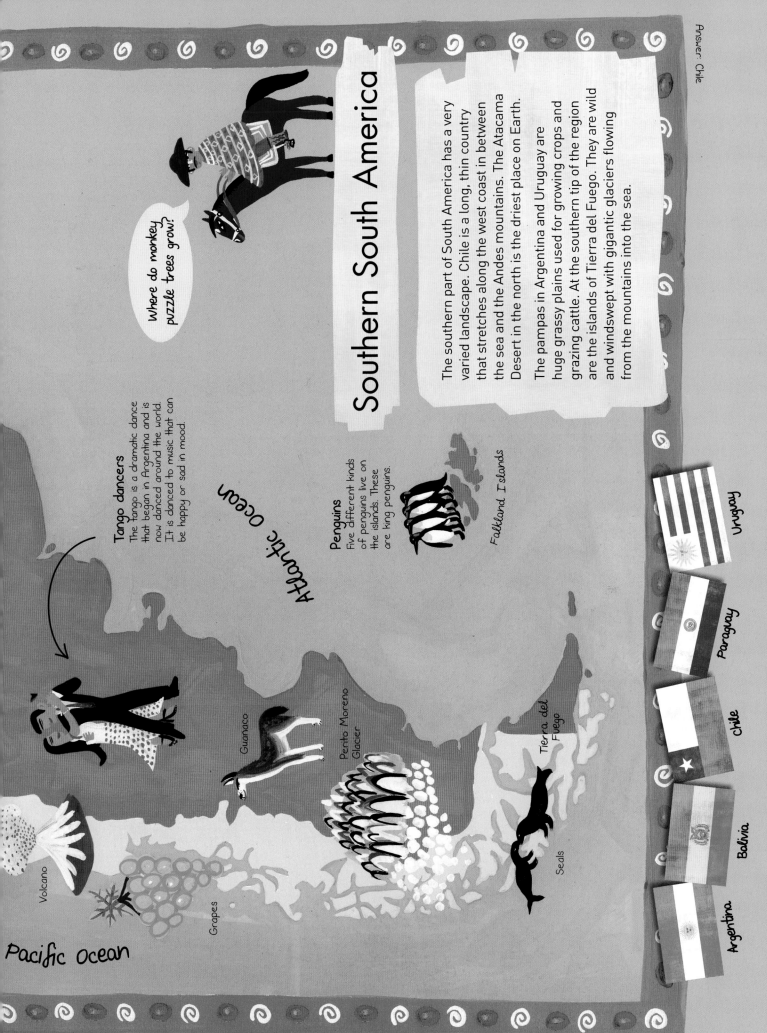

Where do monkey puzzle trees grow?

Tango dancers
The tango is a dramatic dance that began in Argentina and is now danced around the world. It is danced to music that can be happy or sad in mood.

Atlantic Ocean

Penguins
Five different kinds of penguins live on the islands. These are king penguins.

Falkland Islands

Guanaco

Perito Moreno Glacier

Tierra del Fuego

Seals

Volcano

Grapes

Pacific Ocean

Uruguay

Paraguay

Chile

Bolivia

Argentina

Europe

Europe is the world's second smallest continent—only Australia is smaller. Even so, around 750 million people live in Europe. Only Asia and Africa have more people. Europe is made up of many different countries, each with its own culture and, usually, its own language. The biggest country in Europe is Russia. Europe's smallest country is Vatican City in Italy.

ICELAND

SCOTLAND

NORTHERN IRELAND

IRELAND

WALES

ENGLAND

Atlantic Ocean

English Channel

SPAIN

PORTUGAL

ICELAND

★ Reykjavik

Icelandic pony

Sami people
The icy north of Scandinavia is called Lapland. It is home to the Sami people. Some Sami herd reindeer for their meat, milk, and skin.

Orcas

Norwegian Sea

Elk

Ice hotel

Wolf

Ice fishing

RUSSIA

Viking longship
The Vikings lived in Scandinavia about 1,000 years ago. They raided other countries in wooden boats called longships.

Fjords
Hundreds of jagged valleys, called fjords, cut into the coast of Norway. They were carved out by glaciers, then later filled in with sea.

Mythical troll

Rune stone

Kick-sledding

FINLAND

Cattle

SWEDEN

Wooden Dalecarlian toy horse

NORWAY

Air Guitar World Championships

Which colors are in the swedish flag?

Cross-country skier

★ Oslo

Saab

★ Stockholm

★ Helsinki

Little Mermaid statue

Folk dancing

Scandinavia

North Sea

LEGO

DENMARK

★ Copenhagen

Baltic Sea

GERMANY

The most northern part of Europe is called Scandinavia. It is made up of the countries of Norway, Sweden, Finland, Denmark, and Iceland. Thick forests of pine and spruce trees grow in Norway, Sweden, and Finland. Norway has high mountains, but Denmark is a flat country. It is made up of a piece of mainland and lots of small islands. Iceland, an island in the Norwegian Sea, is 915 miles from Norway. It has many active volcanoes and geysers that spurt out hot water and steam.

Scandinavians have a high standard of living. Norway is rich in oil and gas. Sweden and Finland produce lots of timber. Denmark has fertile farmland. It is also the home of LEGO!

Norway

Sweden

Finland

Denmark

Iceland

Answer: Blue and yellow

Shetland pony

Shetland Islands

Golf

Oil tanker

Mythical Loch Ness monster

Highland cow

Bagpipes
The bagpipes are a musical instrument played in Scotland. This player is wearing a kilt, a traditional Scottish garment made from tartan fabric.

Leprechaun
Popular in Irish legends, leprechauns are types of fairies who like making mischief. They are usually shown as old men, about as tall as children.

Atlantic Ocean

Edinburgh

SCOTLAND

NORTHERN IRELAND

Hadrian's Wall

Cricket

North sea

Belfast

Red squirrel

IRELAND

Dublin

Irish harp

WALES

ENGLAND

Welsh Dragon symbol

Corgi

London Eye

Big Ben

Blarney Castle

Kingfisher

Stonehenge
Stonehenge is an ancient circle of stones. It was built more than 4,000 years ago and may have been a temple or burial site.

Cardiff

London

English Channel

Can you find someone playing golf ?

British Isles

The British Isles are made up of the United Kingdom (Scotland, England, Wales, and Northern Ireland) and Ireland. The British Isles are famous for their history and traditions.

Ireland is a separate country to the United Kingdom. It has beautiful countryside and a mild but rainy climate.

United Kingdom

Ireland

Spain and Portugal

Spain and Portugal lie in the southwest corner of Europe on a piece of land that juts out into the sea. The Pyrenees mountains in the north divide these two countries from the rest of Europe. The southern tip of Spain is only a few miles from Africa.

Spain and Portugal have sunny climates, sandy beaches, and flavorful food. This makes them popular spots for vacationers. Spain is also famous for its colorful fiestas (street festivals) and flamenco dancing. In Portugal, fishing along the Atlantic coast is an important industry, and people eat lots of fish and seafood here.

Can you find some golden sunflowers?

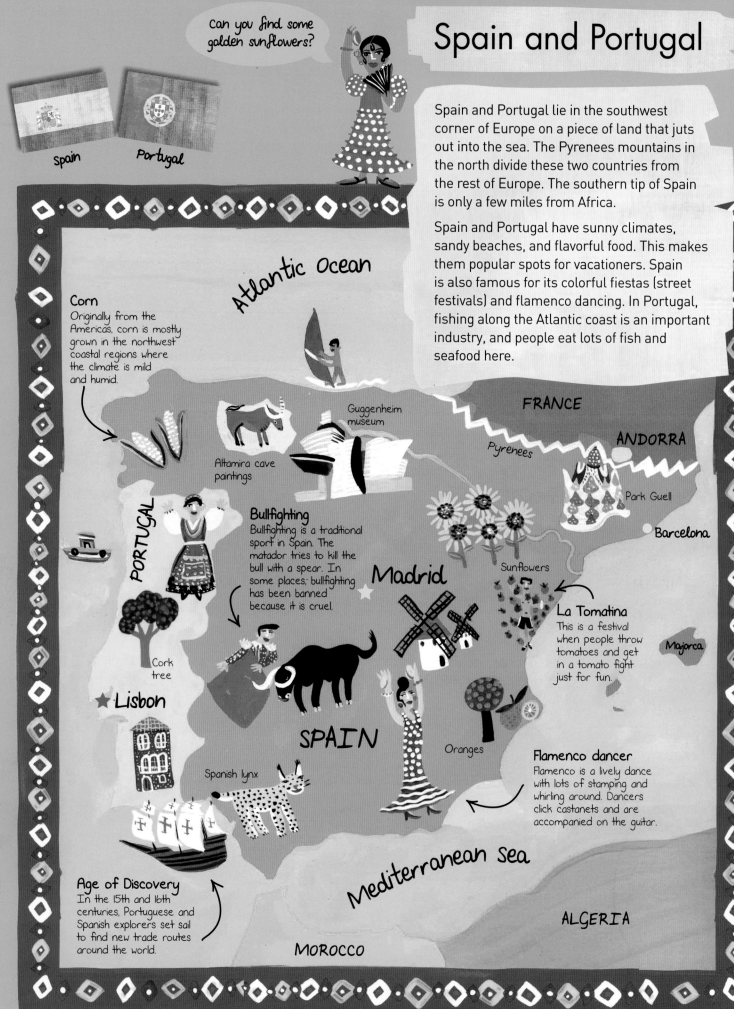

Spain

Portugal

Atlantic Ocean

Corn
Originally from the Americas, corn is mostly grown in the northwest coastal regions where the climate is mild and humid.

Guggenheim museum

Altamira cave paintings

FRANCE

ANDORRA

Pyrenees

Park Guell

Barcelona

PORTUGAL

Bullfighting
Bullfighting is a traditional sport in Spain. The matador tries to kill the bull with a spear. In some places, bullfighting has been banned because it is cruel.

Sunflowers

Madrid

La Tomatina
This is a festival when people throw tomatoes and get in a tomato fight just for fun.

Majorca

Cork tree

Lisbon

SPAIN

Oranges

Flamenco dancer
Flamenco is a lively dance with lots of stamping and whirling around. Dancers click castanets and are accompanied on the guitar.

Spanish lynx

Age of Discovery
In the 15th and 16th centuries, Portuguese and Spanish explorers set sail to find new trade routes around the world.

Mediterranean Sea

ALGERIA

MOROCCO

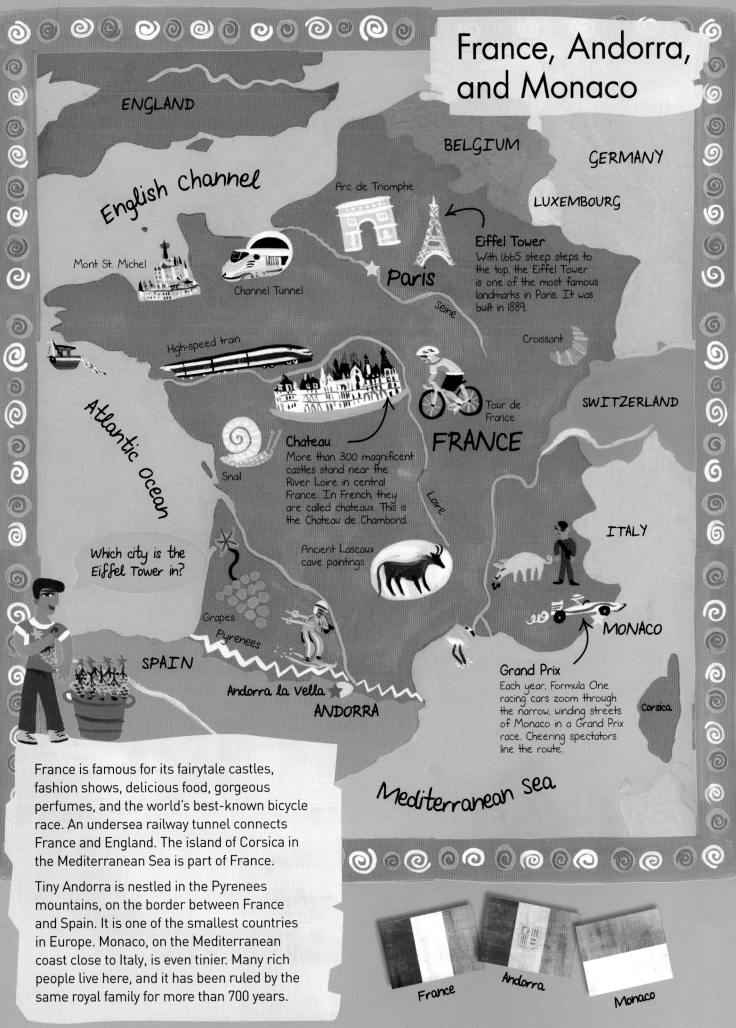

France, Andorra, and Monaco

ENGLAND

English channel

BELGIUM

GERMANY

LUXEMBOURG

Arc de Triomphe

Eiffel Tower
With 1,665 steep steps to the top, the Eiffel Tower is one of the most famous landmarks in Paris. It was built in 1889.

Mont St. Michel

Channel Tunnel

Paris

Seine

Croissant

High-speed train

Atlantic Ocean

Snail

Chateau
More than 300 magnificent castles stand near the River Loire in central France. In French, they are called chateaux. This is the Chateau de Chambord.

Tour de France

FRANCE

Loire

SWITZERLAND

ITALY

Ancient Lascaux cave paintings

Which city is the Eiffel Tower in?

Grapes

Pyrenees

SPAIN

Andorra la Vella

ANDORRA

MONACO

Grand Prix
Each year, Formula One racing cars zoom through the narrow, winding streets of Monaco in a Grand Prix race. Cheering spectators line the route.

Corsica

Mediterranean Sea

France is famous for its fairytale castles, fashion shows, delicious food, gorgeous perfumes, and the world's best-known bicycle race. An undersea railway tunnel connects France and England. The island of Corsica in the Mediterranean Sea is part of France.

Tiny Andorra is nestled in the Pyrenees mountains, on the border between France and Spain. It is one of the smallest countries in Europe. Monaco, on the Mediterranean coast close to Italy, is even tinier. Many rich people live here, and it has been ruled by the same royal family for more than 700 years.

France

Andorra

Monaco

Answer: Paris

Netherlands, Belgium, and Luxembourg

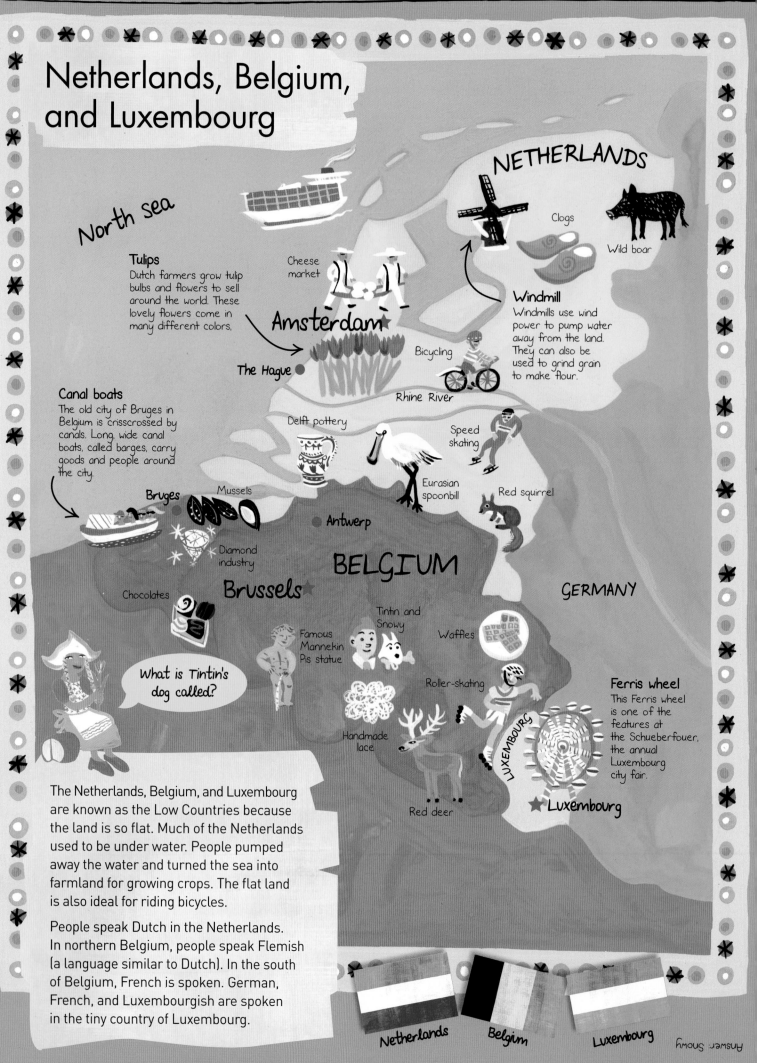

NETHERLANDS

North sea

Tulips
Dutch farmers grow tulip bulbs and flowers to sell around the world. These lovely flowers come in many different colors.

Cheese market

Clogs

Wild boar

Amsterdam

The Hague

Bicycling

Windmill
Windmills use wind power to pump water away from the land. They can also be used to grind grain to make flour.

Rhine River

Canal boats
The old city of Bruges in Belgium is crisscrossed by canals. Long, wide canal boats, called barges, carry goods and people around the city.

Delft pottery

Speed skating

Eurasian spoonbill

Red squirrel

Bruges

Mussels

Antwerp

BELGIUM

GERMANY

Diamond industry

Brussels

Chocolates

Tintin and Snowy

Waffles

Ferris wheel
This Ferris wheel is one of the features at the Schueberfouer, the annual Luxembourg city fair.

Famous Mannekin Pis statue

Roller-skating

What is Tintin's dog called?

Handmade lace

LUXEMBOURG

Red deer

Luxembourg

The Netherlands, Belgium, and Luxembourg are known as the Low Countries because the land is so flat. Much of the Netherlands used to be under water. People pumped away the water and turned the sea into farmland for growing crops. The flat land is also ideal for riding bicycles.

People speak Dutch in the Netherlands. In northern Belgium, people speak Flemish (a language similar to Dutch). In the south of Belgium, French is spoken. German, French, and Luxembourgish are spoken in the tiny country of Luxembourg.

Netherlands   Belgium   Luxembourg

Answer: Snowy

Germany, Switzerland, Liechtenstein, and Austria

North sea

White stork

NETHERLANDS

Timber-frame house

Hamburg

Garden gnome figurine

Dachshund

Nutcracker

Rhine River

Cologne Cathedral

Cologne

GERMANY

Berlin ★

Brandenburg Gate

Dresden porcelain

POLAND

LUXEMBOURG

Red fox

Frankfurt

Neuschwanstein Castle

Lederhosen
Lederhosen are shorts made from leather. They are sometimes worn by men in southern Germany and Austria as part of a traditional costume.

CZECH REPUBLIC

Marmot

Cuckoo clock
Cuckoo clocks were invented in Germany almost 300 years ago. When the clock strikes, a bird pops out and calls "Cuckoo!"

Danube

Munich

Snowboarding

Vienna ★

Swiss cheese

Dentures

AUSTRIA

SWITZERLAND ★ Bern

Vaduz
LIECHTENSTEIN

Sound of Music

Edelweiss

Alps

Lipizzaner horse
Beautiful, graceful Lipizzaner horses take part in dazzling displays at the Spanish Riding School in Vienna, Austria.

St. Bernard

Which two countries border Liechtenstein?

Germany

Switzerland

Liechtenstein

Austria

Germany is a large country in the center of Europe. In the north, it has a border with Denmark. In the south, it has borders with Austria and Switzerland. These two countries are nestled in the Alps, a chain of towering snowcapped mountains. Millions of people visit the Alps each year to ski and snowboard.

Germany, Austria, and Switzerland are wealthy countries. They have lots of factories and industries, making goods such as cars and watches. In Germany, goods are often transported by river or canal on large barges.

Answer: Switzerland and Austria

North Central Europe

Shipbuilding

Smigus-Dyngus
A boy throws water on the girl he likes at the water festival on Easter Monday.

Horse-drawn sleigh

Which country likes to put on puppet shows?

GERMANY

POLAND

Warsaw

Astronomical clock

Prague

CZECH REPUBLIC

Floating to Earth
Stefan Banic, from Slovakia, invented the parachute in 1914. To demonstrate how it worked, he bravely jumped from a 41st-story window.

Brown bear

SLOVAKIA

Czech puppet
Puppets are very popular in the Czech Republic. There are lots of theaters where you can watch puppet shows and shops that sell puppets.

Bratislava

Mythical Turul bird

Budapest

HUNGARY

Fictional Count Dracula

Carpathian Mountains

Pelican

Rubik's Cube

Dried peppers

ROMANIA

Csiko horseman
Csikos are cattle-herders from Hungary. They are skillful horse riders, able to stand on two horses at the same time.

Danube

Gypsy cart

Bucharest

Black Sea

The countries of north central Europe are to the east of Germany and Austria. Most of this region is quite flat, but there are mountains in Slovakia. The great River Danube flows from Germany through Slovakia, Hungary, and Romania before emptying into the Black Sea.

Some of Europe's most historical cities are found in this region. Prague is the capital of the Czech Republic. It is famous for its ancient buildings and bridges. Budapest is the capital of Hungary. It is actually two cities—Buda, on one bank of the River Danube, and Pest, on the other.

Sofia

Bagpipes

BULGARIA

Roses

Yarn Martenitsa dolls worn to welcome spring

Poland   Czech Republic   Slovakia   Hungary   Romania   Bulgaria

Answer: Czech Republic

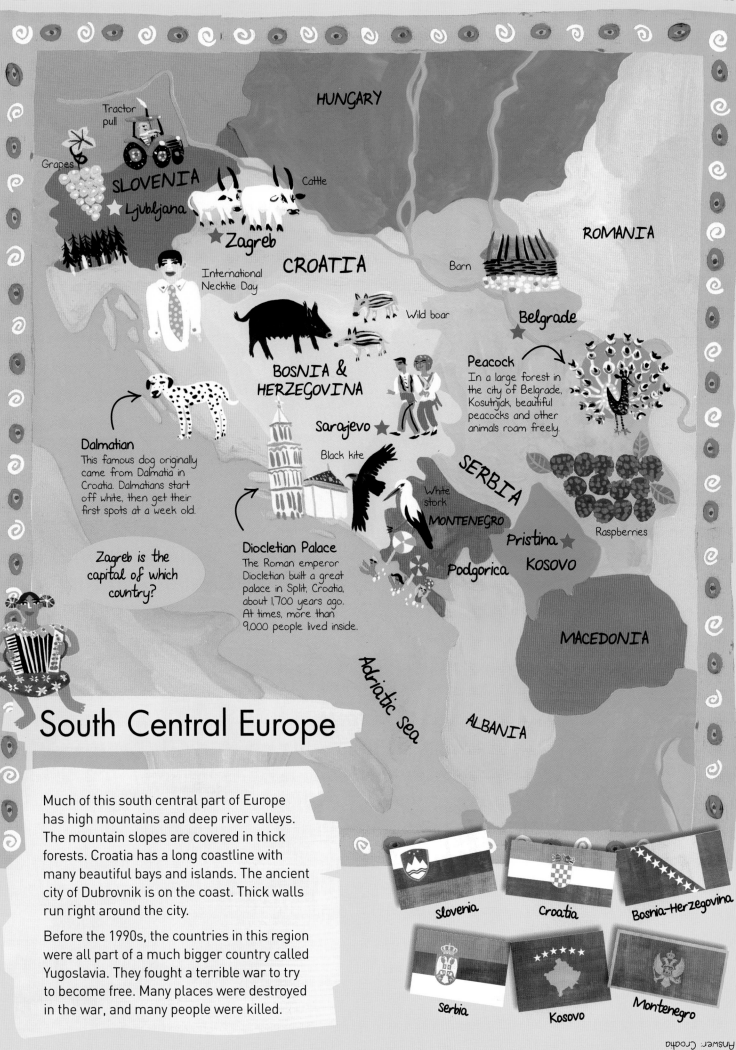

HUNGARY

Tractor pull

Grapes

SLOVENIA

Ljubljana

Cattle

Zagreb

CROATIA

International Necktie Day

ROMANIA

Barn

Belgrade

Wild boar

Peacock

In a large forest in the city of Belgrade, Kosutnjak, beautiful peacocks and other animals roam freely.

BOSNIA & HERZEGOVINA

Sarajevo

Black kite

Dalmatian

This famous dog originally came from Dalmatia in Croatia. Dalmatians start off white, then get their first spots at a week old.

SERBIA

White stork

MONTENEGRO

Raspberries

Pristina

KOSOVO

Podgorica

Zagreb is the capital of which country?

Diocletian Palace

The Roman emperor Diocletian built a great palace in Split, Croatia, about 1,700 years ago. At times, more than 9,000 people lived inside.

MACEDONIA

Adriatic Sea

ALBANIA

South Central Europe

Much of this south central part of Europe has high mountains and deep river valleys. The mountain slopes are covered in thick forests. Croatia has a long coastline with many beautiful bays and islands. The ancient city of Dubrovnik is on the coast. Thick walls run right around the city.

Before the 1990s, the countries in this region were all part of a much bigger country called Yugoslavia. They fought a terrible war to try to become free. Many places were destroyed in the war, and many people were killed.

Slovenia

Croatia

Bosnia-Herzegovina

Serbia

Kosovo

Montenegro

Answer: Croatia

Italy and Southern Europe

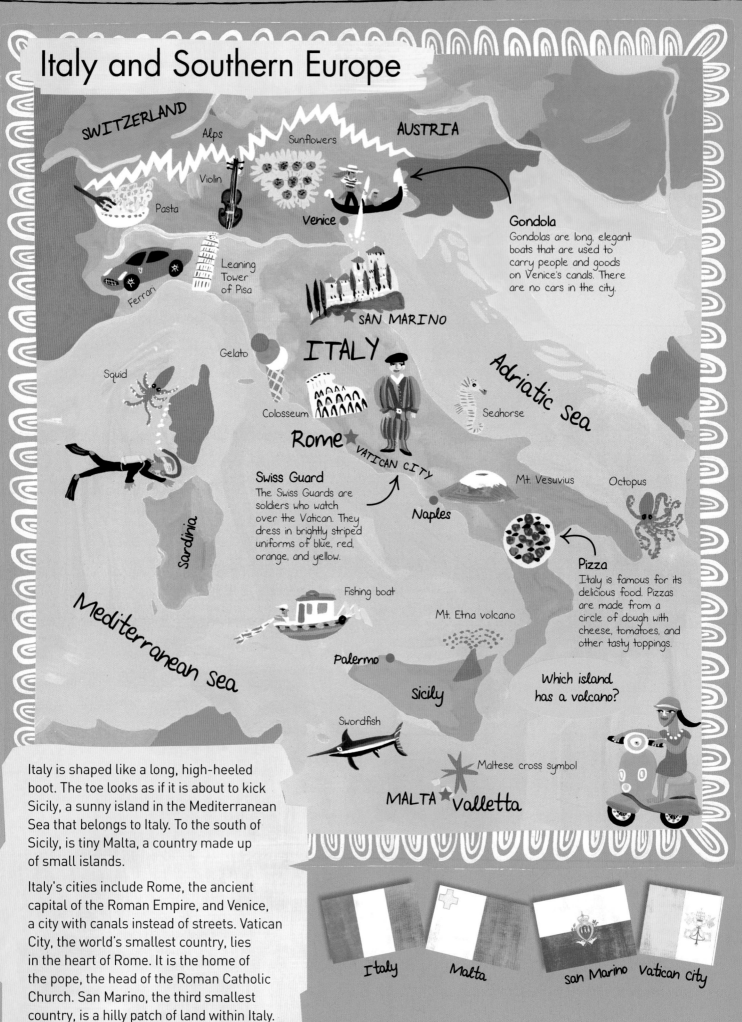

SWITZERLAND

Alps

Sunflowers

AUSTRIA

Violin

Pasta

Venice

Gondola
Gondolas are long, elegant boats that are used to carry people and goods on Venice's canals. There are no cars in the city.

Ferrari

Leaning Tower of Pisa

SAN MARINO

Gelato

ITALY

Squid

Adriatic Sea

Colosseum

Seahorse

Rome

VATICAN CITY

Swiss Guard
The Swiss Guards are soldiers who watch over the Vatican. They dress in brightly striped uniforms of blue, red, orange, and yellow.

Mt. Vesuvius

Octopus

Naples

Sardinia

Pizza
Italy is famous for its delicious food. Pizzas are made from a circle of dough with cheese, tomatoes, and other tasty toppings.

Mediterranean Sea

Fishing boat

Mt. Etna volcano

Palermo

Which island has a volcano?

Sicily

Swordfish

Maltese cross symbol

MALTA Valletta

Italy is shaped like a long, high-heeled boot. The toe looks as if it is about to kick Sicily, a sunny island in the Mediterranean Sea that belongs to Italy. To the south of Sicily, is tiny Malta, a country made up of small islands.

Italy's cities include Rome, the ancient capital of the Roman Empire, and Venice, a city with canals instead of streets. Vatican City, the world's smallest country, lies in the heart of Rome. It is the home of the pope, the head of the Roman Catholic Church. San Marino, the third smallest country, is a hilly patch of land within Italy.

Italy   Malta   San Marino   Vatican City

Albania, Greece, and Macedonia

Two-stringed guitar

Skopje

Corn

MACEDONIA

Eels in Lake Ohrid

Tirana ★

Puppy
Yugoslav shepherd dogs guard sheep in Macedonia. When this puppy grows up, it will be strong enough to fight off wolves.

BULGARIA

Lute

Olives

ALBANIA

Horned cow

Sheep

500 BC painting of a boy playing with a yo-yo

Olympics
The ancient Greeks were the first to hold Olympic games.

Aegean Sea

Pegasus
In Greek mythology, Pegasus was a flying horse with a shining white coat and wings. He was ridden by the hero Bellerophon.

GREECE

Medusa is a monster in Greek mythology.

Evzones guards
Dressed in kilts, red caps and black shoes with pompoms, the Evzones are Greek soldiers who guard the Parliament in Athens.

Parthenon

Adriatic sea

Can you see a cute puppy?

Greek pottery

★ Athens

Greek salad

King Agamemnon's golden funeral mask

The Bull of Crete sculpture

Albania, Greece, and Macedonia are in southeastern Europe where it is hot and dry. Much of the area is mountainous. Greek farmers grow olives on hilly slopes for eating or making into olive oil. Greece has more than 2,000 sun-drenched islands scattered off the coast. Millions of tourists visit every year to see the ruins of ancient Greek cities and buildings.

Macedonia was home to such famous leaders as Alexander the Great and Egypt's Cleopatra. The symbol of Albania is a double-headed eagle, which appears on this rugged country's flag.

Crete

Albania

Greece

Macedonia

Belarus   Estonia   Latvia   Lithuania   Moldova   Ukraine   Russia

Baltic Sea

FINLAND

Walrus

Spotted seal

Fabergé egg

Puffin

POLAND

Warsaw

LATVIA   Riga   ESTONIA   Tallinn

LITHUANIA

Amber

Vilnius

Ladybug

Fallow deer

St. Petersburg

St. Basil's Cathedral
St. Basil's Cathedral is a beautiful church in Moscow's Red Square. Its onion-shaped domes are brightly painted and covered in carvings.

Oil

Minsk

BELARUS

Wisent

Moscow

Ballet

Ural Mountains

Extinct woolly mammoth

Spiders are good luck in Ukraine

Kiev

MOLDOVA   UKRAINE

Chisinau

Easter eggs

Cossack dancer
The Cossacks were bands of soldiers from Ukraine. They are famous for their energetic dancing, which includes acrobatic jumps.

Molnija watch and clockmaker

Ice hockey

Irtysh

Black Sea

Volgograd

Troika

KAZAKHSTAN

Caspian Sea

Trans-Siberian Railroad

The countries of eastern Europe include Estonia, Latvia, and Lithuania. They are known as the Baltic States because they border the Baltic Sea. Belarus, Ukraine, and Moldova are to the south. To the east is Russia, the world's biggest country. Russia and its neighbors were once part of an even bigger country called the Soviet Union.

Russia is so enormous that it stretches from Europe across Asia. It would take two months of nonstop walking to go from one end to the other. Most people live in cities in the west, including the capital city, Moscow.

Baltic States and Russia

Matryoshka doll
Russian matryoshka dolls are a set of wooden dolls that get smaller and smaller. They are placed inside each other in order of size.

Arctic Ocean

Polar bears

Arctic fox

Indigenous Yakut

Wolf

RUSSIA

Chess

Oil

Volcano

Horseback riding

Gymnastics

Kamchatka Peninsula

Siberian house

Reindeer sleigh

Salmon

Irkutsk

Lake Baikal

Siberian tiger

Pacific Ocean

Which mountains are in Russia?

MONGOLIA

Vladivostok

Asia

Asia is truly enormous—the largest continent on Earth. Covering almost a third of Earth's land area, it stretches from the Arctic in the north to the Equator in the south, and from the Mediterranean Sea in the west to the Pacific Ocean in the east. Asia has 48 countries and is home to more than 3.8 billion people—about two out of every three of us on the planet.

Middle East

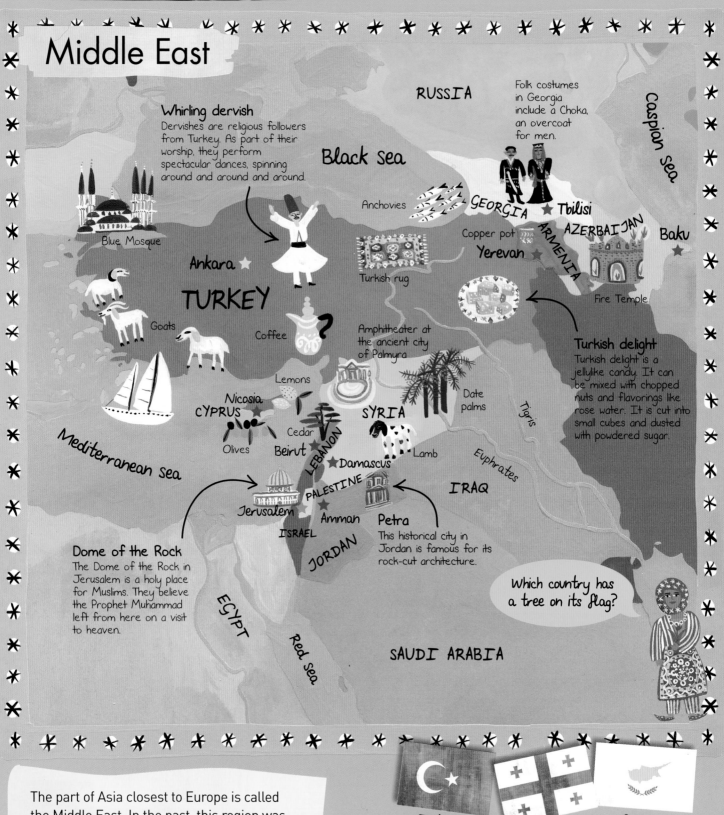

Whirling dervish
Dervishes are religious followers from Turkey. As part of their worship, they perform spectacular dances, spinning around and around and around.

Folk costumes in Georgia include a Choka, an overcoat for men.

RUSSIA

Black Sea

Anchovies

GEORGIA Tbilisi

Caspian Sea

Copper pot AZERBAIJAN

ARMENIA

Yerevan Baku

Blue Mosque

Ankara

TURKEY

Turkish rug

Fire Temple

Goats

Coffee

Turkish delight
Turkish delight is a jellylike candy. It can be mixed with chopped nuts and flavorings like rose water. It is cut into small cubes and dusted with powdered sugar.

Lemons

Amphitheater at the ancient city of Palmyra

Date palms

Tigris

Nicosia
CYPRUS

SYRIA

Cedar

Euphrates

Olives Beirut

LEBANON

Lamb

Mediterranean sea

Damascus

IRAQ

PALESTINE

Jerusalem

Amman

Petra

Petra
This historical city in Jordan is famous for its rock-cut architecture.

ISRAEL

JORDAN

Dome of the Rock
The Dome of the Rock in Jerusalem is a holy place for Muslims. They believe the Prophet Muhammad left from here on a visit to heaven.

EGYPT

Which country has a tree on its flag?

Red sea

SAUDI ARABIA

The part of Asia closest to Europe is called the Middle East. In the past, this region was an important crossroads for trade between three continents—Europe, Asia, and Africa. Turkey is the largest country in the region. It lies mostly in Asia with a small part in Europe. Its biggest city, Istanbul, is the only city in the world that sits in two continents.

Many people in the Middle East are Muslims. They follow the religion of Islam. Two other great religions—Judaism and Christianity—also began in the region.

Turkey

Georgia

Cyprus

Armenia

Azerbaijan

Syria

Lebanon

Israel

Jordan

Answer: Lebanon

Middle East

Caspian Sea

Sturgeon

Cotton

Iraq

Iran

Tigris

Euphrates

Samarra Mosque

Mashhad

Tehran

Turquoise

Stone carvings at the ancient city of Persepolis

Leopard

Sheep

Baghdad

IRĀQ

IRAN

Barley

Ziggurat of Ur

KUWAIT

Kuwait city

Arabian horse

Persian Gulf

Wild cat
The caracal is a small wild cat that lives in Iran and other parts of Asia. It has long, black, tufty ears. It uses its razor-sharp claws and teeth to catch prey, such as hares and gazelles.

Oyster

Date palms

SAUDI ARABIA

Oil

Bedouins

Oil tanker

Manama

BAHRAIN

Burj Khalifa

QATAR

Doha

Abu Dhabi

Muscat

Coral reef

Riyadh

Scorpion

UNITED ARAB EMIRATES

Oryx

Tiger shark

Falcon

OMAN

Red Sea

Mecca

Coconuts

Arabian Sea

Grand Mosque
Each year, millions of Muslims travel to Mecca to visit the Grand Mosque. Inside the mosque stands a cube-shaped shrine called the Kaaba. This is the holiest place for Muslims.

Apricots

Barracuda

Sanaa

YEMEN

Camel racing
For thousands of years, camel racing has been a popular sport in Saudi Arabia. Hundreds of riders take part in the biggest races, hoping to win a cash prize.

Sand cat

Where can you find an oryx?

Most of Saudi Arabia is covered by baking hot, dry desert. In the west is the city of Mecca, which is holy for Muslims. They believe this is where the Prophet Muhammad was born and began teaching people about Islam. Wherever Muslims are in the world, they face toward Mecca when they pray.

Some of the countries in the Middle East, such as Saudi Arabia, Kuwait, and Qatar, have large oil supplies. They sell their oil around the world. This has made them very wealthy.

Saudi Arabia

Kuwait

Qatar

Bahrain

United Arab Emirates

Oman

Yemen

Answer: Oman

Kazakhstan

Kyrgyzstan

Tajikistan

Turkmenistan

Uzbekistan

RUSSIA

Traditional tent
Many people in Central Asia traditionally lived as nomads. They moved from place to place with their animals. They lived in tents, called yurts, that were quick and easy to put up and take down.

Marmot

Apple trees

Riders on horseback

Boat stranded in sand near the shrinking Aral Sea

Aral Sea

Caspian sea

Bowl of caviar

Folk costume

UZBEKISTAN

Mausoleum in Samarkand

TURKMENISTAN

Cotton plant

Colorful rug

Marwari horse

Sheep

★ Ashgabat

IRAN

AFGHANISTAN

Central Asia

Gold reserves

Irtysh

Snow leopard
Snow leopards are very rare big cats that live high up in the mountains in Central Asia. They are well suited to living in the cold, with long, thick fur, stocky bodies, and small, round ears.

★ Astana

KAZAKHSTAN

Rocket on launchpad

Spoonbill

Watermelon

Lake Balkhash

Tien Shan Mountains

CHINA

Wild boars

What is the capital of Turkmenistan?

Tashkent

★ Bishkek
KYRGYZSTAN

Yak

Yak
Yaks are strong, sturdy animals with shaggy fur that protects them from the bitter mountain cold. They are also extremely smelly because their thick fur traps dirt and germs.

TAJIKISTAN
★ Dushanbe

Central Asia lies to the southwest of Russia and was ruled by Russia until 1991. In the north are huge, grass-covered plains called steppes. In the center are two vast, dry deserts. The south is bordered by snowcapped mountains.

Kazakhstan is the biggest country in Central Asia. Mining is important in the country. It also has large stores of oil and gas. The Baikonur Space Center is in the center of Kazakhstan. Many space rockets and satellites are launched from here every year.

Answer: Ashgabat

Afghanistan and Pakistan

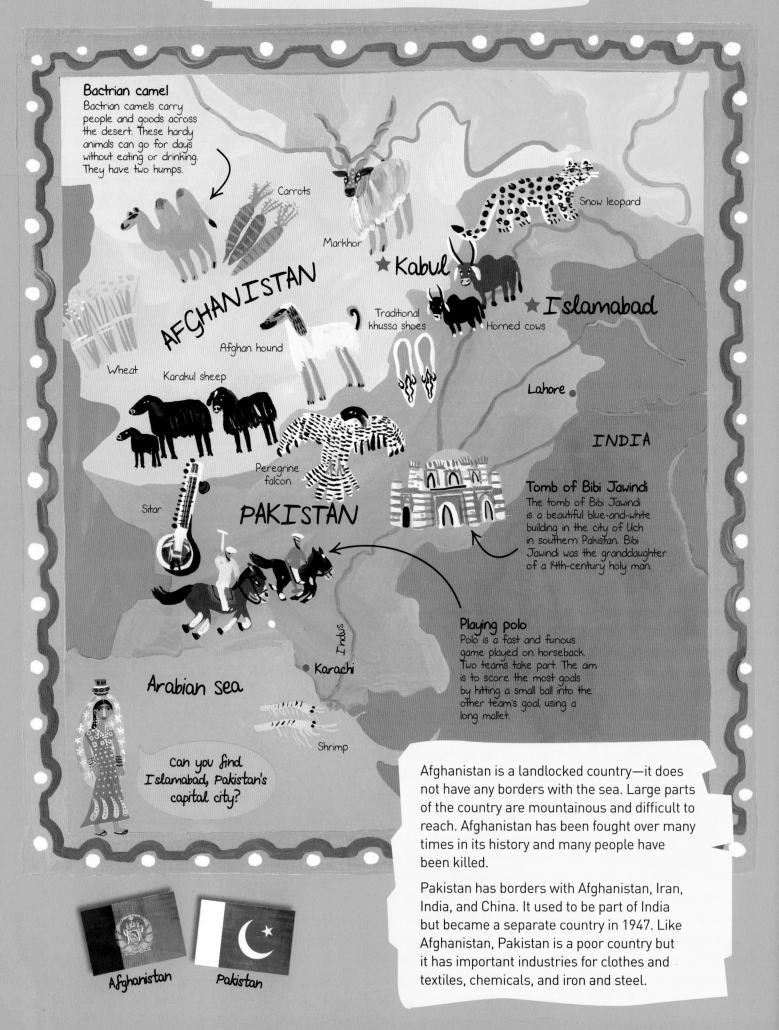

Bactrian camel
Bactrian camels carry people and goods across the desert. These hardy animals can go for days without eating or drinking. They have two humps.

Carrots

Markhor

Snow leopard

★ Kabul

★ Islamabad

AFGHANISTAN

Traditional khussa shoes

Horned cows

Afghan hound

Wheat

Karakul sheep

Lahore

INDIA

Peregrine falcon

Sitar

PAKISTAN

Tomb of Bibi Jawindi
The tomb of Bibi Jawindi is a beautiful blue-and-white building in the city of Uch in southern Pakistan. Bibi Jawindi was the granddaughter of a 14th-century holy man.

Playing polo
Polo is a fast and furious game played on horseback. Two teams take part. The aim is to score the most goals by hitting a small ball into the other team's goal, using a long mallet.

Indus

Karachi

Arabian sea

Shrimp

Can you find Islamabad, Pakistan's capital city?

Afghanistan is a landlocked country—it does not have any borders with the sea. Large parts of the country are mountainous and difficult to reach. Afghanistan has been fought over many times in its history and many people have been killed.

Pakistan has borders with Afghanistan, Iran, India, and China. It used to be part of India but became a separate country in 1947. Like Afghanistan, Pakistan is a poor country but it has important industries for clothes and textiles, chemicals, and iron and steel.

Afghanistan   Pakistan

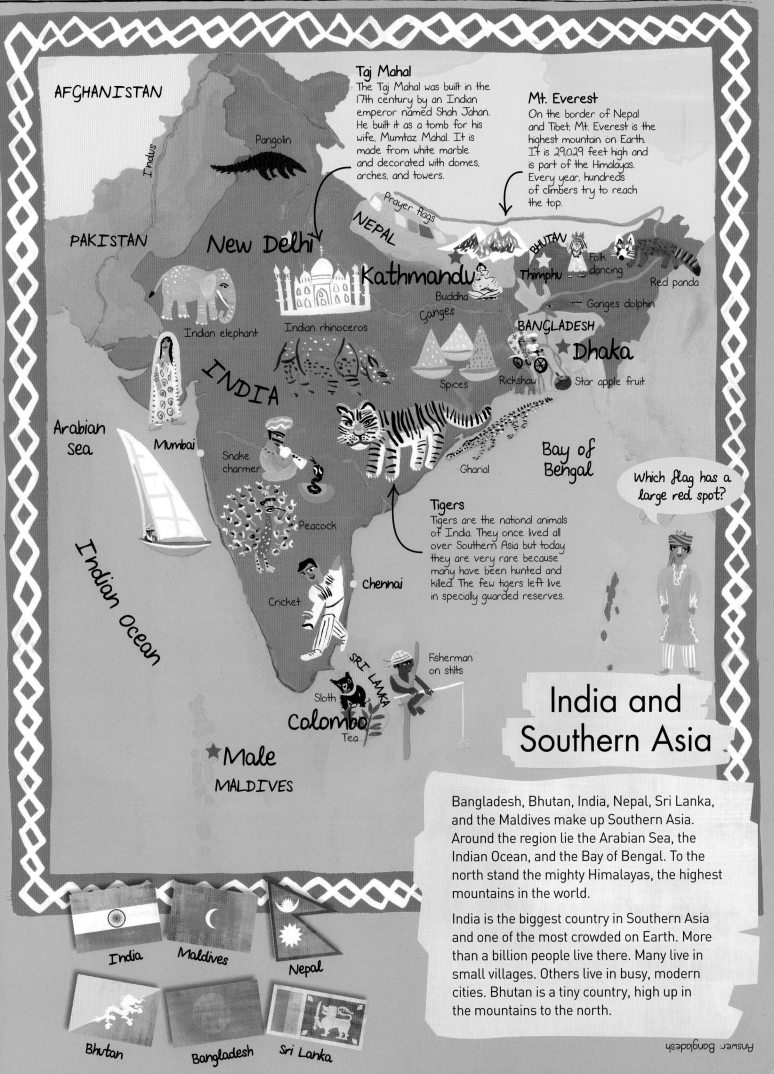

AFGHANISTAN

Indus

Pangolin

Taj Mahal
The Taj Mahal was built in the 17th century by an Indian emperor named Shah Jahan. He built it as a tomb for his wife, Mumtaz Mahal. It is made from white marble and decorated with domes, arches, and towers.

Mt. Everest
On the border of Nepal and Tibet, Mt. Everest is the highest mountain on Earth. It is 29,029 feet high and is part of the Himalayas. Every year, hundreds of climbers try to reach the top.

PAKISTAN

New Delhi

Prayer flags

NEPAL

Kathmandu

BHUTAN

Thimphu

Folk dancing

Red panda

Indian elephant

Indian rhinoceros

Buddha

Ganges

Ganges dolphin

BANGLADESH

Dhaka

Mumbai

INDIA

Spices

Rickshaw

Star apple fruit

Arabian Sea

Snake charmer

Peacock

Tigers

Gharial

Bay of Bengal

Which flag has a large red spot?

Tigers
Tigers are the national animals of India. They once lived all over Southern Asia but today they are very rare because many have been hunted and killed. The few tigers left live in specially guarded reserves.

Chennai

Cricket

Indian Ocean

SRI LANKA

Fisherman on stilts

Sloth

Colombo

Tea

Male

MALDIVES

India and Southern Asia

Bangladesh, Bhutan, India, Nepal, Sri Lanka, and the Maldives make up Southern Asia. Around the region lie the Arabian Sea, the Indian Ocean, and the Bay of Bengal. To the north stand the mighty Himalayas, the highest mountains in the world.

India is the biggest country in Southern Asia and one of the most crowded on Earth. More than a billion people live there. Many live in small villages. Others live in busy, modern cities. Bhutan is a tiny country, high up in the mountains to the north.

India

Maldives

Nepal

Bhutan

Bangladesh

Sri Lanka

Answer: Bangladesh

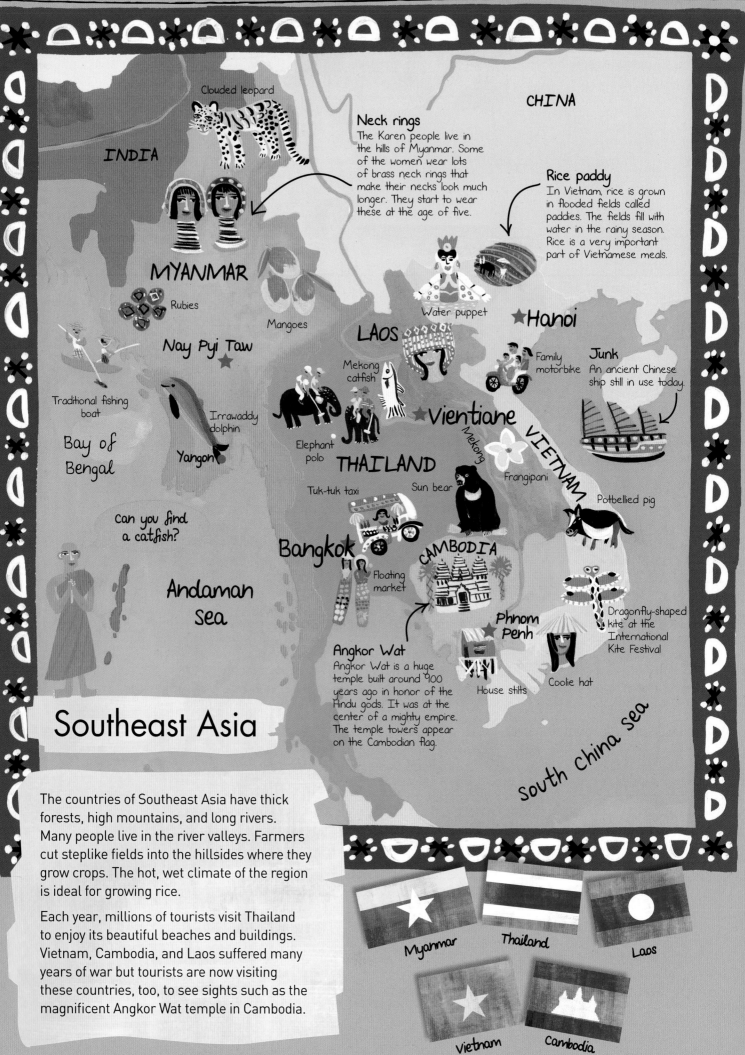

CHINA

Clouded leopard

INDIA

Neck rings
The Karen people live in the hills of Myanmar. Some of the women wear lots of brass neck rings that make their necks look much longer. They start to wear these at the age of five.

Rice paddy
In Vietnam, rice is grown in flooded fields called paddies. The fields fill with water in the rainy season. Rice is a very important part of Vietnamese meals.

MYANMAR

Rubies

Mangoes

Water puppet

★ Hanoi

Nay Pyi Taw

LAOS

Mekong catfish

Family motorbike

Junk
An ancient Chinese ship still in use today.

Traditional fishing boat

Irrawaddy dolphin

Elephant polo

★ Vientiane

VIETNAM

Bay of Bengal

Yangon

THAILAND

Mekong

Frangipani

Potbellied pig

Tuk-tuk taxi

Sun bear

Can you find a catfish?

Bangkok

Floating market

CAMBODIA

Phnom Penh

Dragonfly-shaped kite at the International Kite Festival

Andaman Sea

Angkor Wat
Angkor Wat is a huge temple built around 900 years ago in honor of the Hindu gods. It was at the center of a mighty empire. The temple towers appear on the Cambodian flag.

House stilts

Coolie hat

South China Sea

Southeast Asia

The countries of Southeast Asia have thick forests, high mountains, and long rivers. Many people live in the river valleys. Farmers cut steplike fields into the hillsides where they grow crops. The hot, wet climate of the region is ideal for growing rice.

Each year, millions of tourists visit Thailand to enjoy its beautiful beaches and buildings. Vietnam, Cambodia, and Laos suffered many years of war but tourists are now visiting these countries, too, to see sights such as the magnificent Angkor Wat temple in Cambodia.

Myanmar

Thailand

Laos

Vietnam

Cambodia

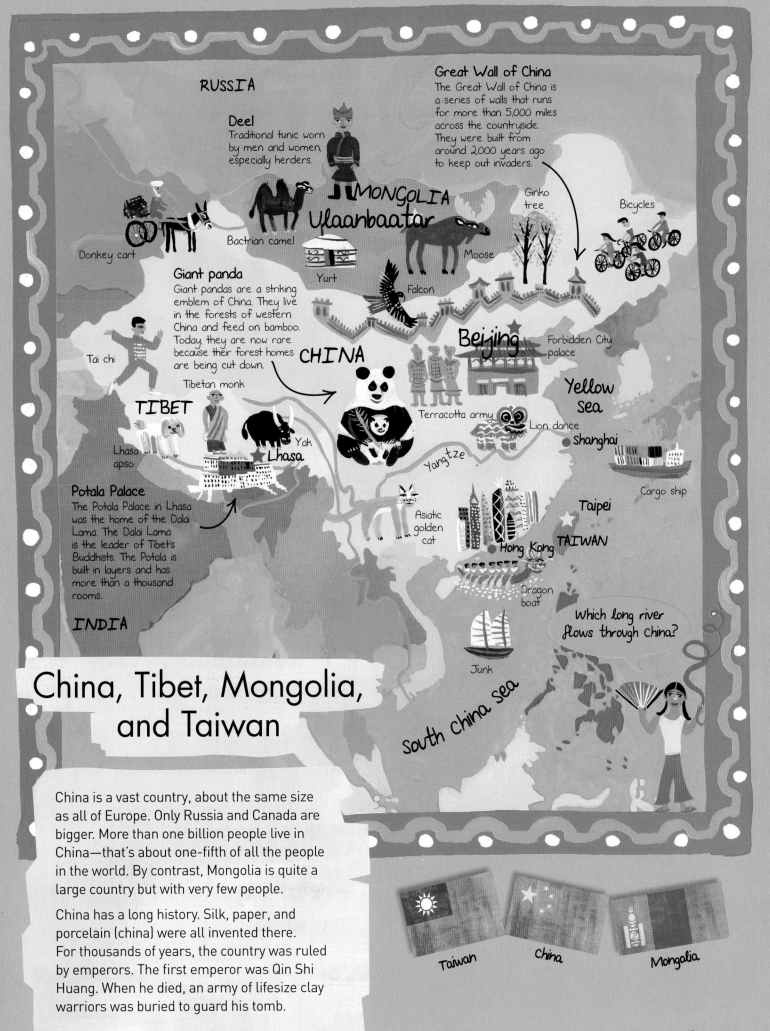

RUSSIA

Deel
Traditional tunic worn by men and women, especially herders.

Great Wall of China
The Great Wall of China is a series of walls that runs for more than 5,000 miles across the countryside. They were built from around 2,000 years ago to keep out invaders.

MONGOLIA
Ulaanbaatar

Bactrian camel

Donkey cart

Yurt

Ginko tree

Bicycles

Moose

Falcon

Giant panda
Giant pandas are a striking emblem of China. They live in the forests of western China and feed on bamboo. Today, they are now rare because their forest homes are being cut down.

Tai chi

Tibetan monk

CHINA

Beijing

Forbidden City palace

Yellow Sea

TIBET

Lhasa apso

Yak

Lhasa

Terracotta army

Lion dance

Shanghai

Yangtze

Cargo ship

Potala Palace
The Potala Palace in Lhasa was the home of the Dalai Lama. The Dalai Lama is the leader of Tibet's Buddhists. The Potala is built in layers and has more than a thousand rooms.

Asiatic golden cat

Taipei

Hong Kong

TAIWAN

INDIA

Dragon boat

Which long river flows through china?

Junk

South china sea

China, Tibet, Mongolia, and Taiwan

China is a vast country, about the same size as all of Europe. Only Russia and Canada are bigger. More than one billion people live in China—that's about one-fifth of all the people in the world. By contrast, Mongolia is quite a large country but with very few people.

China has a long history. Silk, paper, and porcelain (china) were all invented there. For thousands of years, the country was ruled by emperors. The first emperor was Qin Shi Huang. When he died, an army of lifesize clay warriors was buried to guard his tomb.

Taiwan

China

Mongolia

North and South Korea

North Korea

South Korea

The Korean Peninsula is a piece of land in Asia that juts out into the Pacific Ocean. It is split into two countries—North Korea and South Korea. Both have high mountains and thick forests. In winter, the weather is bitterly cold. In summer, it can be very hot and sticky.

North Korea has a strict government that does not allow much contact with the outside world. South Korea is much more open. It trades with many other countries, including Japan and the USA, selling products such as computers, cars, and electronic goods.

Traditional hanbok dress

Mythical Chollima

Cargo ship

Magnolia blossom

Sino-Korean Friendship Bridge

CHINA

NORTH KOREA

Dear Leader statue

Farmer carrying grain

Pyongyang

Gymnastics

Gymnastics are popular in North Korea. On national holidays, tens of thousands of gymnasts take part in huge displays. Young gymnasts spend months and years in training.

Sea of Japan

Gyeongbokgung Palace

Ice sculpture

Every winter, ice festivals are held in cities around North Korea. The festivals feature spectacular ice sculptures that take many months to make.

Seoul

SOUTH KOREA

Octopus

Hibiscus flower

Fan dancers

Women dancers in South Korea perform spectacular fan dances. As they dance, they move faster and faster, making patterns of flowers, butterflies, and waves with their fans.

Grandfather stone sculpture

Yellow Sea

Swordfish

Hyundai car

KTX high-speed train

Pusan

Squid

JAPAN

Can you see a hibiscus flower?

Tae kwon do

CHINA

RUSSIA

NORTH KOREA

SOUTH KOREA

Sea of Japan

Pacific Ocean

Skier

Macaque

Hokkaido

Mako shark

Japanese crane

Origami

Origami means "paper folding" and is a traditional Japanese art. Experts can make complicated models of animals, objects, and shapes out of simple sheets of paper.

Sushi

Sushi is a famous Japanese dish. It is made up of small pieces of raw fish, seaweed, and rice. Japanese people eat more fish and seafood than anyone else in the world.

Puffer fish

Kabuki theater

Manga

Woman wearing kimono

Sumo wrestler

Sumo is Japanese wrestling. Wrestlers are very heavy and have to train hard at special sumo schools. They try to throw each other out of a circular ring called a dohyo.

Himeji Castle

JAPAN Honshu

Pagoda

Mt. Fuji

Tokyo

Torii gate

Osaka

Cherry blossom

Pearl diver

Traditional wasen fishing boat

What is the capital of Japan?

Japan

Japan is a chain of thousands of islands in East Asia. Most people live on the four biggest islands—Hokkaido, Honshu, Shikoku, and Kyushu. The countryside is hilly with not much land left for farming and building on, so many people live in cities by the coast. The capital city is Tokyo, one of the busiest and biggest cities in the world.

Japan is a modern, wealthy country, but traditions are still very important. At special times, people wear traditional long-sleeved robes called kimonos and wooden sandals.

Japan

Answer: Tokyo

Malaysia

Singapore

Brunei

Indonesia

East Timor

Philippines

CHINA

South China Sea

Palawan

Malay lacewing butterfly

Clown fish

Petronas Twin Towers

MALAYSIA

Bandar Seri Begawan

BRUNEI

Orangutan

Kuala Lumpur

Medan

Merlion fountain

House on stilts

Tiger shark

Sail-tail lizard

Sumatra

Singapore

SINGAPORE

Rafflesia flower

Sumatran tiger

Borneo

Indian Ocean

Flying fish

Traditional long house

Hunter with blowpipe

Proboscis monkey

INDONESIA

Jakarta

Sumatran rhino
The Sumatran rhino lives in Sumatra, Borneo, and Malaysia. It is very rare. It is hunted for its horns, which are used in Chinese medicine.

Can you find five types of fish?

Java

Surabaya

Seahorse

Shadow puppets
In Indonesia, shadow puppets are used to tell stories from myths and holy books. The puppets are made from buffalo leather. Their shadows are cast onto a white cloth.

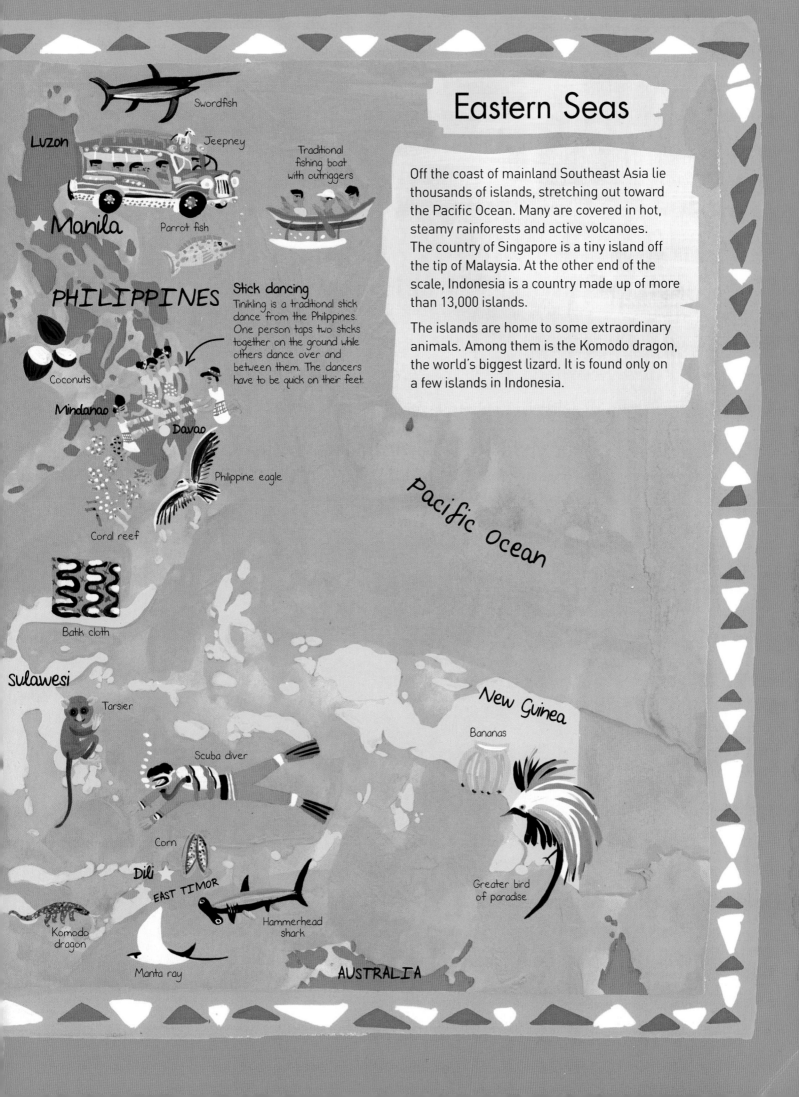

Eastern Seas

Off the coast of mainland Southeast Asia lie thousands of islands, stretching out toward the Pacific Ocean. Many are covered in hot, steamy rainforests and active volcanoes. The country of Singapore is a tiny island off the tip of Malaysia. At the other end of the scale, Indonesia is a country made up of more than 13,000 islands.

The islands are home to some extraordinary animals. Among them is the Komodo dragon, the world's biggest lizard. It is found only on a few islands in Indonesia.

Swordfish

Luzon

Jeepney

Traditional fishing boat with outriggers

Manila

Parrot fish

PHILIPPINES

Stick dancing
Tinikling is a traditional stick dance from the Philippines. One person taps two sticks together on the ground while others dance over and between them. The dancers have to be quick on their feet.

Coconuts

Mindanao

Davao

Philippine eagle

Coral reef

Batik cloth

Sulawesi

Tarsier

Scuba diver

Corn

Dili

EAST TIMOR

Komodo dragon

Hammerhead shark

Manta ray

AUSTRALIA

Pacific Ocean

New Guinea

Bananas

Greater bird of paradise

Oceania

Oceania is made up of Australia—the world's smallest continent—New Zealand, Papua New Guinea, and hundreds of tiny islands that are scattered over a huge area of the Pacific Ocean. The region has many different types of landscapes, from tropical rainforests and coral reefs to volcanoes and glaciers. Some 35 million people live in Oceania.

PALAU

AUSTRALIA

FEDERATED STATES
OF MICRONESIA

MARSHALL
ISLANDS

NAURU

KIRIBATI

Pacific Ocean

PAPUA
NEW GUINEA

TUVALU

SOLOMON
ISLANDS

SAMOA

VANUATU

FIJI

Coral
Sea

NEW
CALEDONIA

TONGA

Tasman Sea

NEW ZEALAND

Indian Ocean

Pacific Ocean

Leafy seadragon

Uluru
Uluru (Ayers Rock) is a massive block of sandstone about 1,150 feet tall. It is a sacred place for the Aboriginal people. Caves at the base of the rock are decorated with ancient paintings.

Oyster with pearl

Aboriginal man playing didgeridoo

Crocodile

Giant termite mound

Great Barrier Reef
The Great Barrier Reef is the world's largest coral reef. It stretches for more than 1,600 miles and is home to a huge number of creatures, including more than 1,500 species of fish.

Boomerang

Rock paintings

Emu

Tropical rain forest

Echidna

Brown snake

AUSTRALIA

Dingo

Koala

Brisbane

Herding sheep

Gray kangaroo

Sydney Opera House

Perth

Thorny devil

Opals

Australian Rules football

Superb lyrebird

Sydney

Canberra

Red kangaroo
Like many of Australia's famous animals, red kangaroos are marsupials. Females carry their young in their pouch. Kangaroos move about by hopping on their large back feet, using their tail for balance.

Tiger shark

Dugong

Blue-ringed octopus

Pilot whale

Melbourne

Tram

Surfer

Tasmanian devil

Apples

Australia

Australia is by far the biggest country in Oceania, almost the size of the USA. More than 22 million people live in Australia, mostly in cities along the coasts. Most of the center of Australia is covered in vast stretches of hot, dry desert called the Outback.

The first people to live in Australia were the Aboriginal people about 50,000 years ago. They believe that, at the beginning of time, the landscape was carved out by animal spirits. Today, most Australians are descended from European settlers.

Australia

Where is the city of Perth?

Papua New Guinea and Solomon Islands

Papua New Guinea lies to the north of Australia. It is made up of the eastern end of the island of New Guinea. (The western end of New Guinea is part of Indonesia.) To the east are hundreds of islands called the Solomon Islands.

There are many different groups of people in Papua New Guinea, speaking more than 800 local languages. Each group has its own style of art, dance, and music. Many people are very poor. They live in small, isolated villages and farm the land.

can you find a bird-wing butterfly?

Spirit house, the most important building in a village

Clown fish

Tree kangaroo
Tree kangaroos live in the rainforests of Papua New Guinea. They are great climbers, using their strong front legs to hold on to a tree trunk and their long tails for balance.

Pacific Ocean

Rabaul

Seashells

Traditional dancer

Spike-nosed tree frog

Queen Alexandra's bird-wing butterfly

Volcano

PAPUA NEW GUINEA

SOLOMON ISLANDS

Honiara

Port Moresby

Coral reef

Tropical fish

Mud masks
At festival time, the Asaro mud men of Papua New Guinea cover their bodies in mud and their faces with large clay masks. Traditionally, this is how they frightened off enemies.

House on stilts
In some parts of the Solomon Islands, people build their houses on stilts over the water. The houses are usually made of wood and thatched with palm leaves.

Coral Sea

Papua New Guinea

Solomon Islands

New Zealand and the Pacific

Kiwi fruit

Boiling mud with geyser at Rotorua

Tasman Sea

Kiwi
The national emblem of New Zealand is the kiwi. About the size of a hen, it has a long beak for sniffing out food and cannot fly. It is found only in New Zealand.

Auckland

NEW ZEALAND

Sheep

Barracuda

Giant tree fern

Wellington

Maori dancer
The Maori were the first people to live in New Zealand more than a thousand years ago. As part of their culture, they sometimes paint their faces and perform a war dance called a haka.

Rock climbing

Southern Alps

Fur seals

Blue whale

Pacific Ocean

Hiker

Greenstone charm

Tuatara

Where does kiwi fruit grow?

New Zealand

Fiji

Samoa

Tonga

Vanuatu

Scattered across the southwestern Pacific Ocean lie thousands of islands. New Zealand is made up of two large islands—North and South Island—and lots of smaller ones. North and South Island are separated by the Cook Strait. North Island is warm and mild, with volcanoes and hot springs. South Island has high mountains and glaciers.

Many of the Pacific islands are the tops of volcanoes. Others are coral islands. Many islanders still live traditional lives, growing crops and fishing in the sea.

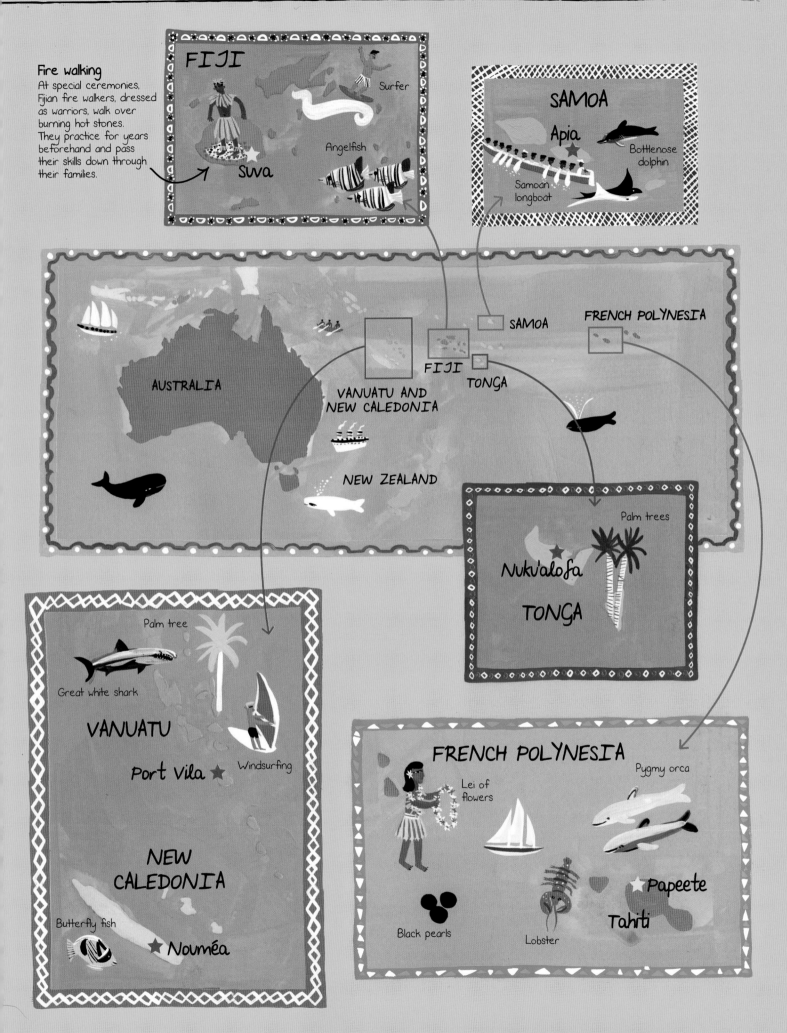

Fire walking
At special ceremonies, Fijian fire walkers, dressed as warriors, walk over burning hot stones. They practice for years beforehand and pass their skills down through their families.

FIJI

Surfer

Angelfish

Suva

SAMOA

Apia

Bottlenose dolphin

Samoan longboat

AUSTRALIA

VANUATU AND NEW CALEDONIA

FIJI

TONGA

SAMOA

FRENCH POLYNESIA

NEW ZEALAND

Palm trees

Nuku'alofa

TONGA

VANUATU

Palm tree

Great white shark

Port Vila

Windsurfing

NEW CALEDONIA

Butterfly fish

Nouméa

FRENCH POLYNESIA

Lei of flowers

Pygmy orca

Black pearls

Lobster

Papeete

Tahiti

Africa

Africa is the second largest continent. It contains more than 50 countries. The biggest is Algeria, which stretches from the Mediterranean coast in the north to deep into the Sahara—the world's biggest desert—in the south. Africa has an amazing landscape. As well as desert, it has rainforest in the center, grasslands in the south, and lakes and mountains along the east.

Red Sea

Mediterranean Sea

EGYPT

LIBYA

TUNISIA

NIGER

ALGERIA

MALI

MOROCCO

MAURITANIA

ERITREA
DJIBOUTI
SOMALIA
ETHIOPIA
KENYA
SUDAN
SOUTH SUDAN
UGANDA
RWANDA
BURUNDI
TANZANIA
MALAWI
MOZAMBIQUE
COMOROS
MADAGASCAR
Indian Ocean
CENTRAL AFRICAN REPUBLIC
CHAD
DEMOCRATIC REPUBLIC OF CONGO
Congo
ZAMBIA
ZIMBABWE
SWAZILAND
LESOTHO
SOUTH AFRICA
BOTSWANA
NAMIBIA
ANGOLA
CONGO
GABON
NIGERIA
CAMEROON
EQUATORIAL GUINEA
SAO TOME & PRINCIPE
BENIN
TOGO
BURKINA FASO
GHANA
IVORY COAST
LIBERIA
SIERRA LEONE
GUINEA
GUINEA-BISSAU
GAMBIA

Atlantic Ocean

CAPE VERDE

SEYCHELLES

MAURITIUS
Reunion

North and West Africa

The vast Sahara covers a large part of northern Africa. This desert can be baking hot by day and freezing cold at night. Despite these harsh conditions, many people and animals live in the desert.

The great River Nile is probably the world's longest river. It begins in Central Africa and flows north through 10 countries, including Egypt, then into the Mediterranean Sea.

Nigeria is an important country in West Africa. It has large supplies of oil and minerals and also grows oil palms and groundnuts.

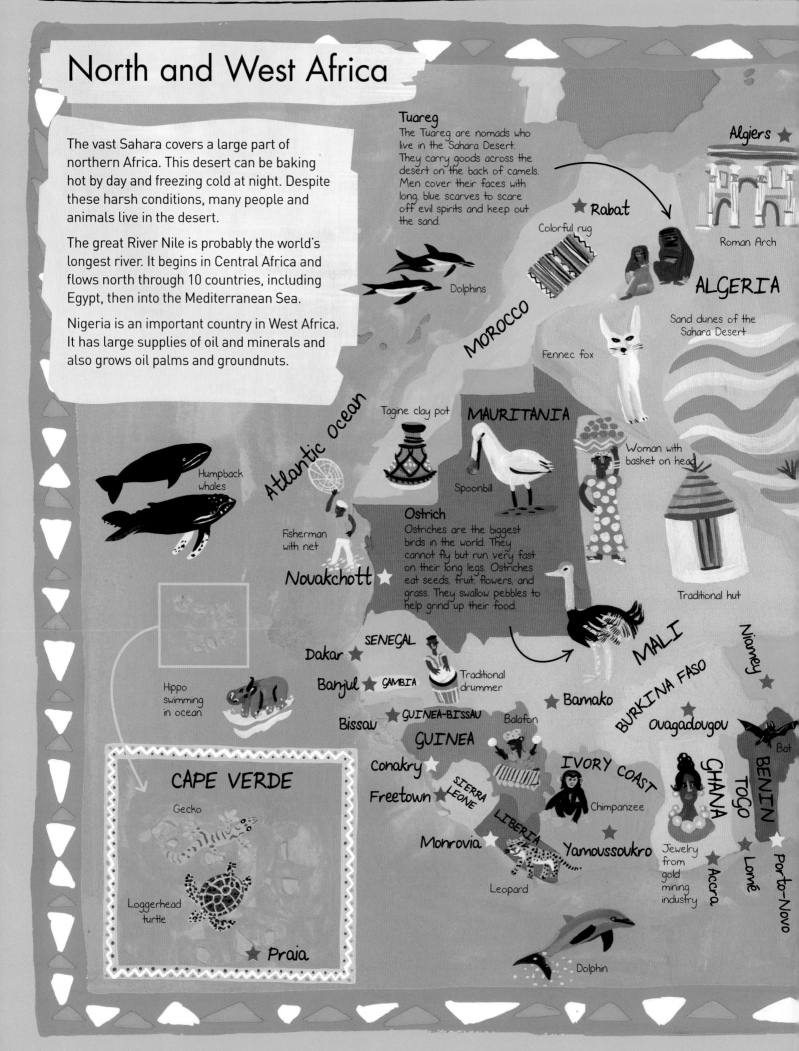

Tuareg
The Tuareg are nomads who live in the Sahara Desert. They carry goods across the desert on the back of camels. Men cover their faces with long, blue scarves to scare off evil spirits and keep out the sand.

Algiers ★

Roman Arch

★ Rabat

Colorful rug

ALGERIA

Sand dunes of the Sahara Desert

MOROCCO

Fennec fox

Dolphins

Atlantic Ocean

Tagine clay pot

MAURITANIA

Woman with basket on head

Spoonbill

Traditional hut

Humpback whales

Fisherman with net

Novakchott ★

Ostrich
Ostriches are the biggest birds in the world. They cannot fly but run very fast on their long legs. Ostriches eat seeds, fruit, flowers, and grass. They swallow pebbles to help grind up their food.

Niamey ★

MALI

SENEGAL ★

Dakar ★

BURKINA FASO

Banjul ★   GAMBIA

Traditional drummer

★ Bamako

Ougadougou ★

Hippo swimming in ocean

Bissau ★   GUINEA-BISSAU

Balafon

GUINEA

IVORY COAST

GHANA

TOGO

BENIN

Bat

Conakry ★

CAPE VERDE

Gecko

Freetown ★   SIERRA LEONE

Chimpanzee

LIBERIA

Monrovia ★

Yamoussoukro ★

Jewelry from gold mining industry

Acra ★

Lomé ★

Porto-Novo

Loggerhead turtle

Leopard

Dolphin

★ Praia

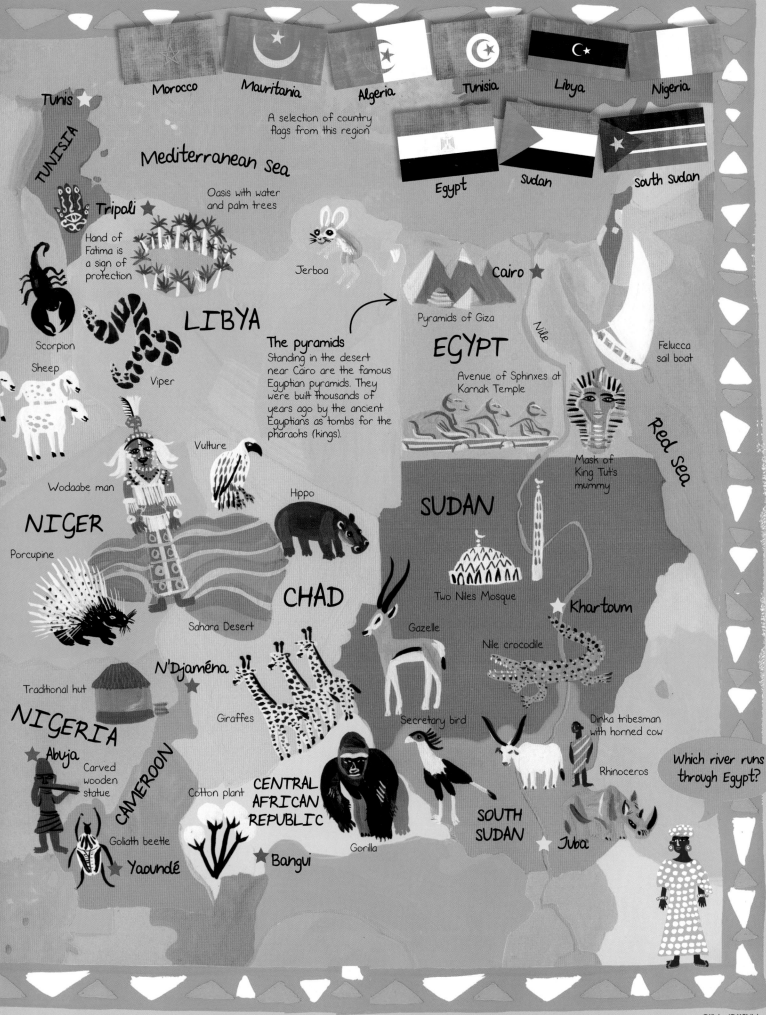

Tunis ★

TUNISIA

Morocco   Mauritania   Algeria   Tunisia   Libya   Nigeria

A selection of country flags from this region

Egypt   Sudan   South Sudan

Mediterranean sea

Oasis with water and palm trees

Tripoli ★

Hand of Fatima is a sign of protection

Jerboa

Cairo ★

Scorpion

Pyramids of Giza

Sheep

LIBYA

Viper

The pyramids
Standing in the desert near Cairo are the famous Egyptian pyramids. They were built thousands of years ago by the ancient Egyptians as tombs for the pharaohs (kings).

EGYPT

Nile

Felucca sail boat

Avenue of Sphinxes at Karnak Temple

Vulture

Wodaabe man

Mask of King Tut's mummy

Red Sea

NIGER

Hippo

Porcupine

SUDAN

Two Niles Mosque

CHAD

Sahara Desert

Gazelle

Khartoum ★

Nile crocodile

N'Djaména ★

Giraffes

Traditional hut

Secretary bird

Dinka tribesman with horned cow

NIGERIA

Abuja ★

Carved wooden statue

CAMEROON

Cotton plant

CENTRAL AFRICAN REPUBLIC

Goliath beetle

Yaoundé ★

Bangui ★

Gorilla

SOUTH SUDAN

Juba ★

Rhinoceros

Which river runs through Egypt?

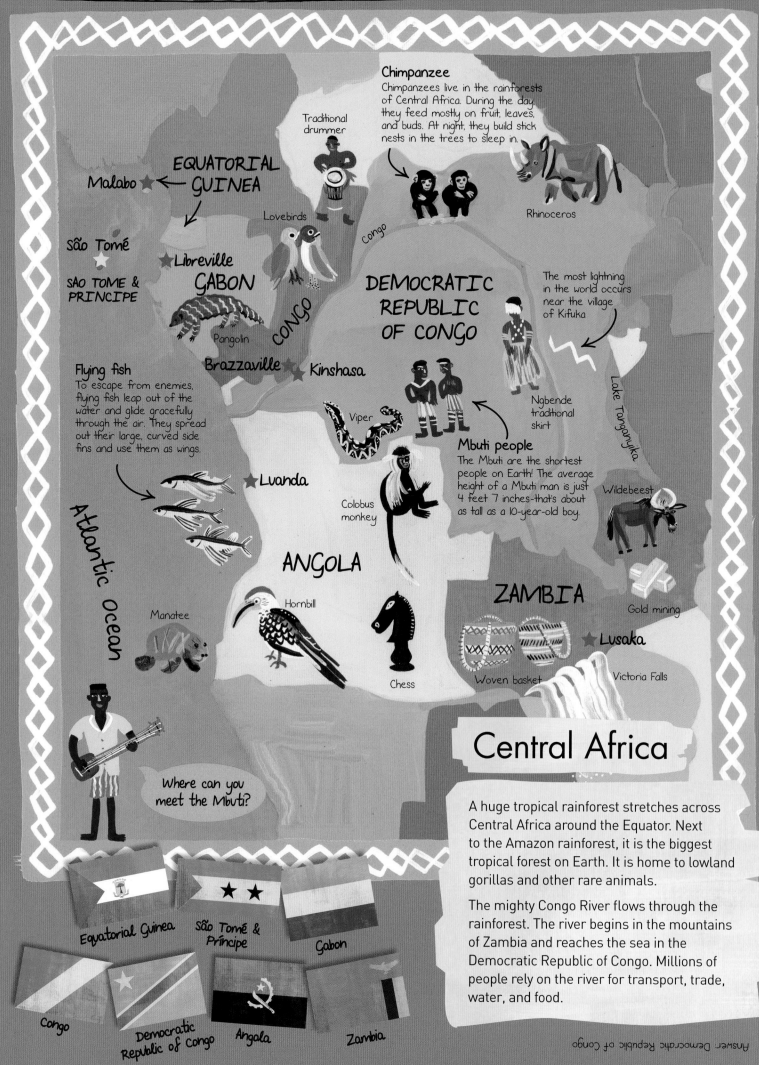

Chimpanzee

Chimpanzees live in the rainforests of Central Africa. During the day, they feed mostly on fruit, leaves, and buds. At night, they build stick nests in the trees to sleep in.

Traditional drummer

EQUATORIAL GUINEA

Malabo

Lovebirds

São Tomé

SAO TOME & PRINCIPE

Libreville

GABON

Pangolin

Rhinoceros

The most lightning in the world occurs near the village of Kifuka

Congo

DEMOCRATIC REPUBLIC OF CONGO

CONGO

Brazzaville

Kinshasa

Lake Tanganyika

Ngbende traditional skirt

Flying fish

To escape from enemies, flying fish leap out of the water and glide gracefully through the air. They spread out their large, curved side fins and use them as wings.

Viper

Mbuti people

The Mbuti are the shortest people on Earth! The average height of a Mbuti man is just 4 feet 7 inches—that's about as tall as a 10-year-old boy.

Luanda

Colobus monkey

Wildebeest

Atlantic ocean

ANGOLA

Manatee

Hornbill

ZAMBIA

Gold mining

Chess

Lusaka

Woven basket

Victoria Falls

Where can you meet the Mbuti?

Central Africa

A huge tropical rainforest stretches across Central Africa around the Equator. Next to the Amazon rainforest, it is the biggest tropical forest on Earth. It is home to lowland gorillas and other rare animals.

The mighty Congo River flows through the rainforest. The river begins in the mountains of Zambia and reaches the sea in the Democratic Republic of Congo. Millions of people rely on the river for transport, trade, water, and food.

Equatorial Guinea

São Tomé & Príncipe

Gabon

Congo

Democratic Republic of Congo

Angola

Zambia

Answer: Democratic Republic of Congo

East Africa

The countries of East Africa stretch from Eritrea in the north to Malawi in the south. A great crack in Earth's crust runs through the region. It is called the Great Rift Valley. A line of lakes fills the valley. There are also high mountains and volcanoes.

Kenya and Tanzania are famous for their wildlife. Huge herds of grazing animals, such as zebras and giraffes, live on the grasslands, together with lions, cheetahs, and elephants. Thousands of people visit the region to go on safari — a wildlife-watching trip.

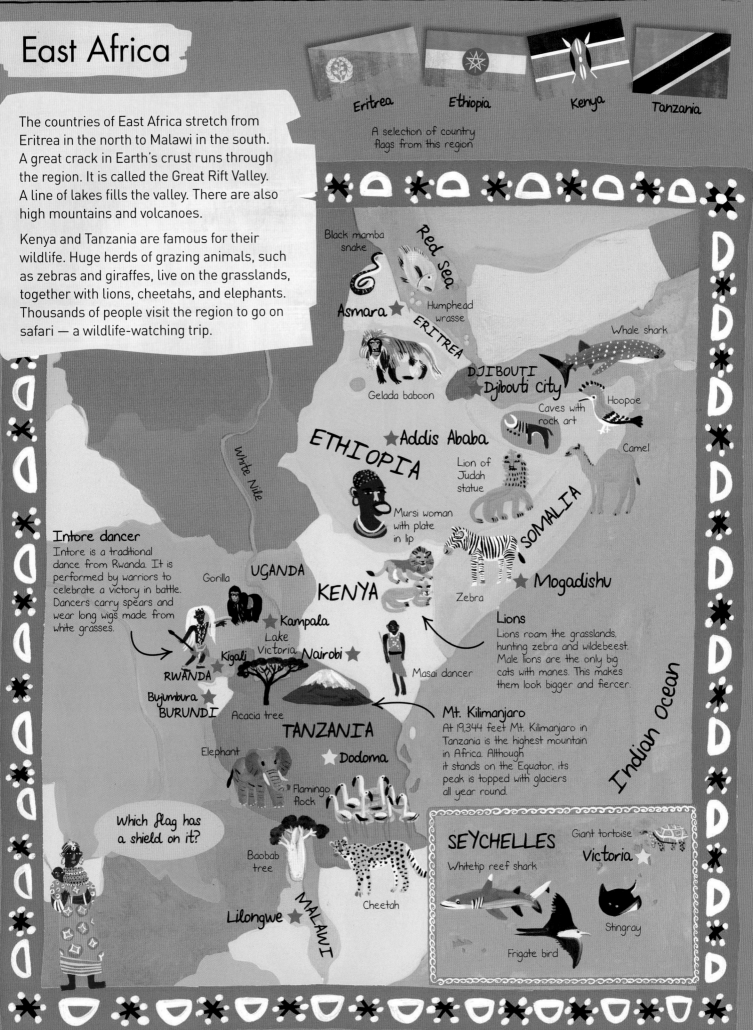

Eritrea   Ethiopia   Kenya   Tanzania

A selection of country flags from this region

Black mamba snake

Red Sea

Asmara

Humphead wrasse

ERITREA

Whale shark

DJIBOUTI
Djibouti city

Gelada baboon

Caves with rock art

Hoopoe

Camel

ETHIOPIA

Addis Ababa

Lion of Judah statue

SOMALIA

Mursi woman with plate in lip

Intore dancer

Intore is a traditional dance from Rwanda. It is performed by warriors to celebrate a victory in battle. Dancers carry spears and wear long wigs made from white grasses.

Gorilla

UGANDA

KENYA

Zebra

Mogadishu

Kampala

Lake Victoria

Nairobi

Kigali

RWANDA

Masai dancer

Lions

Lions roam the grasslands, hunting zebra and wildebeest. Male lions are the only big cats with manes. This makes them look bigger and fiercer.

Bujumbura
BURUNDI

Acacia tree

White Nile

TANZANIA

Mt. Kilimanjaro

At 19,344 feet Mt. Kilimanjaro in Tanzania is the highest mountain in Africa. Although it stands on the Equator, its peak is topped with glaciers all year round.

Elephant

Dodoma

Flamingo flock

Indian Ocean

Which flag has a shield on it?

Baobab tree

SEYCHELLES

Giant tortoise

Victoria

Whitetip reef shark

Cheetah

Lilongwe

MALAWI

Stingray

Frigate bird

Answer: Kenya's

Namibia Botswana Zimbabwe Swaziland South Africa Lesotho

Victoria Falls
The Victoria Falls is a huge waterfall on the Zambezi River where the river plunges off a cliff. Local people call it the "smoke that thunders" because of the sound of the water crashing down.

Traditional canoe

Herero woman

Oryx antelope

Elephant family

Harare ★

ZIMBABWE

Bushman with bow and arrow

Ruins of Great Zimbabwe

Makua tribesman on stilts

NAMIBIA

Kalahari Desert

BOTSWANA

Giraffe

Aardvark

Windhoek ★

Zulu warrior

Meerkats

Gaborone ★

Maputo ★

★ **Pretoria**

Mbabane ★

SWAZILAND

Atlantic Ocean

Namib Desert with long sand dunes

Springbok

Safari jeep

Maseru ★

LESOTHO

Diamonds
South Africa is a world leader in diamond mining. There are seven large diamond mines in the country where diamonds are dug out of the rocks. South Africa is also rich in gold.

SOUTH AFRICA

Dugong

Ndebele woman

● Cape Town

Shrimp

Great white shark

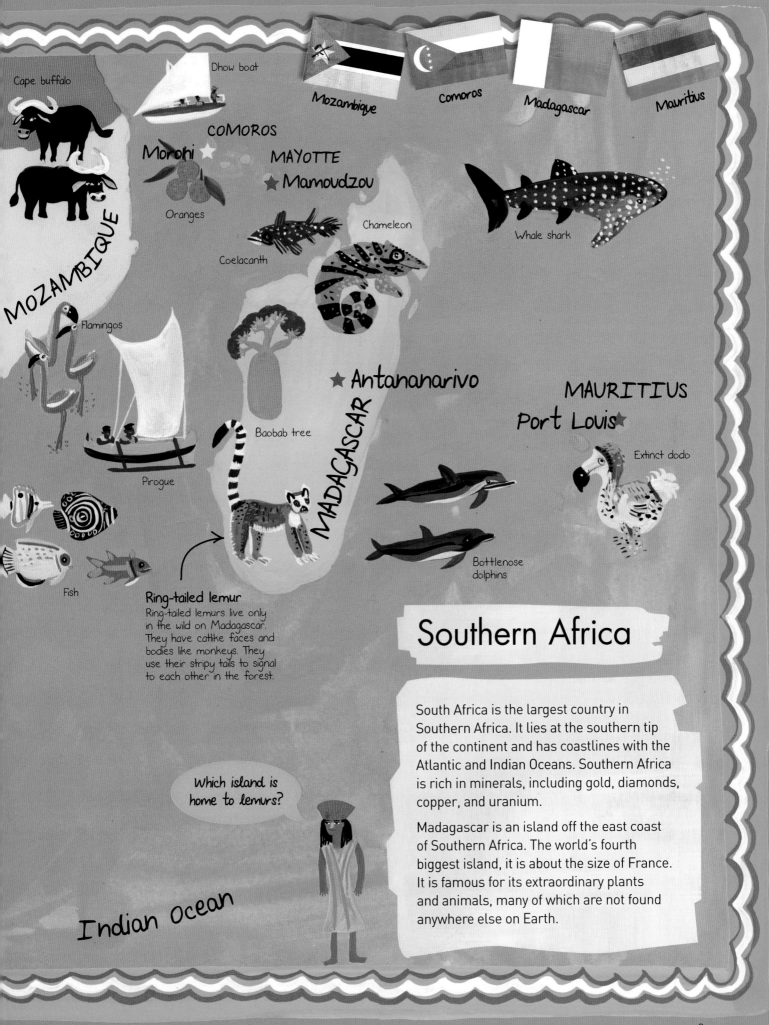

Cape buffalo

Dhow boat

Mozambique

Comoros

Madagascar

Mauritius

COMOROS

Moroni ★

Oranges

MAYOTTE

★ Mamoudzou

MOZAMBIQUE

Coelacanth

Chameleon

Whale shark

Flamingos

Baobab tree

★ Antananarivo

MAURITIUS

Port Louis ★

MADAGASCAR

Extinct dodo

Pirogue

Bottlenose
dolphins

Fish

Ring-tailed lemur
Ring-tailed lemurs live only
in the wild on Madagascar.
They have catlike faces and
bodies like monkeys. They
use their stripy tails to signal
to each other in the forest.

Which island is
home to lemurs?

Southern Africa

South Africa is the largest country in
Southern Africa. It lies at the southern tip
of the continent and has coastlines with the
Atlantic and Indian Oceans. Southern Africa
is rich in minerals, including gold, diamonds,
copper, and uranium.

Madagascar is an island off the east coast
of Southern Africa. The world's fourth
biggest island, it is about the size of France.
It is famous for its extraordinary plants
and animals, many of which are not found
anywhere else on Earth.

Indian Ocean

Answer: Madagascar

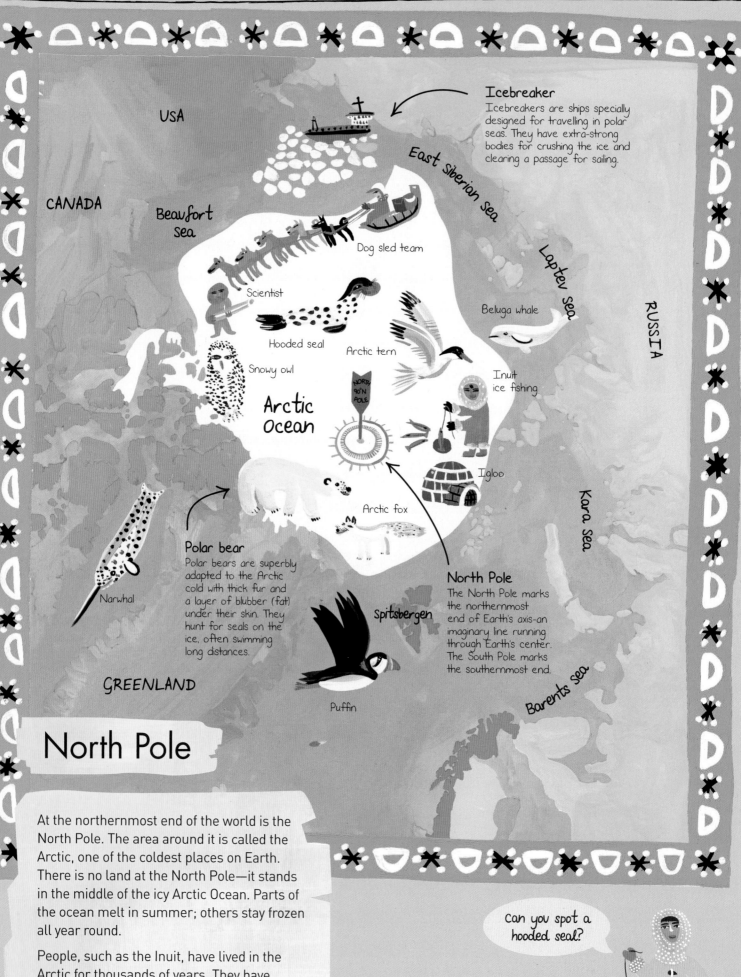

USA

CANADA

Beaufort Sea

East Siberian Sea

Laptev Sea

RUSSIA

Kara Sea

Barents sea

Icebreaker
Icebreakers are ships specially designed for travelling in polar seas. They have extra-strong bodies for crushing the ice and clearing a passage for sailing.

Dog sled team

Scientist

Hooded seal

Arctic tern

Snowy owl

Arctic Ocean

NORTH 90°N POLE

Beluga whale

Inuit ice fishing

Igloo

Arctic fox

Narwhal

Polar bear
Polar bears are superbly adapted to the Arctic cold with thick fur and a layer of blubber (fat) under their skin. They hunt for seals on the ice, often swimming long distances.

Spitsbergen

North Pole
The North Pole marks the northernmost end of Earth's axis—an imaginary line running through Earth's center. The South Pole marks the southernmost end.

GREENLAND

Puffin

North Pole

At the northernmost end of the world is the North Pole. The area around it is called the Arctic, one of the coldest places on Earth. There is no land at the North Pole—it stands in the middle of the icy Arctic Ocean. Parts of the ocean melt in summer; others stay frozen all year round.

People, such as the Inuit, have lived in the Arctic for thousands of years. They have learned to survive in the cold conditions, hunting wild animals, such as seals, for food.

Can you spot a hooded seal?

South Pole

The South Pole is in the middle of Antarctica, a continent almost twice the size of Europe. Most of Antarctica is covered in a thick sheet of ice. Buried beneath the ice are mountains, valleys, and volcanoes. Antarctica is surrounded by the stormy Southern Ocean. In winter, some of the sea freezes, doubling the size of the continent.

The only people on Antarctica are scientists from countries around the world. They live on bases dotted across the continent and study the unique climate, ice, landscape, and wildlife.

How many penguins can you find?

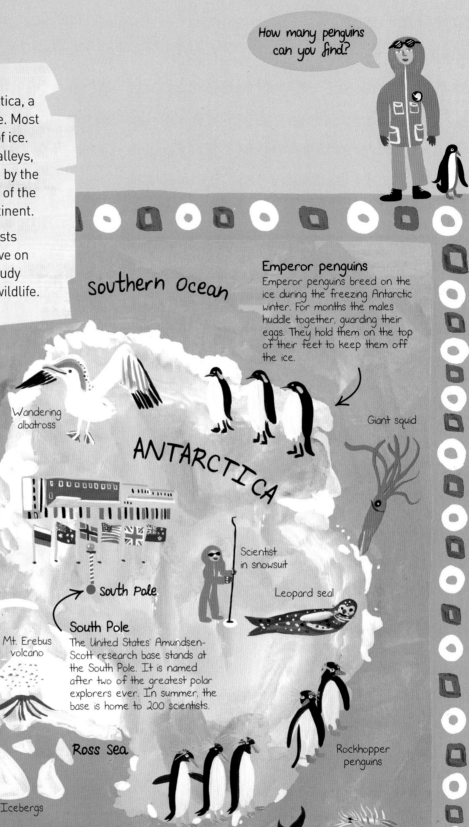

Southern Ocean

Emperor penguins
Emperor penguins breed on the ice during the freezing Antarctic winter. For months the males huddle together, guarding their eggs. They hold them on the top of their feet to keep them off the ice.

Humpback whale

Wandering albatross

Weddell sea

ANTARCTICA

Giant squid

Ski plane

Scientist in snowsuit

Cruise ship

Snow tractor

South Pole

Leopard seal

South Pole
The United States' Amundsen-Scott research base stands at the South Pole. It is named after two of the greatest polar explorers ever. In summer, the base is home to 200 scientists.

Skua

Mt. Erebus volcano

Ice shelf
Enormous shelves of ice stretch out to sea. Huge chunks of ice break off the shelves to form icebergs. In places, the ice shelves are also melting as the world is getting warmer.

Icebergs

Ross Sea

Rockhopper penguins

Orcas

Macaroni penguins with colorful crests

Krill

Southern Ocean

Blue whale

Answer: Eight

Arctic Ocean

NORTH POLE↗

NORTH AMERICA

North Sea

Atlantic Ocean

Pacific Ocean

Caribbean Sea

SOUTH AMERICA

Atlantic Ocean

The World

Planet Earth, the world we live on, is one of eight planets that circle around the sun. More than two-thirds of our world is covered in water—in the oceans, seas, rivers, and lakes. The rest is dry land, divided into seven main chunks, called continents. These are Asia, Africa, North America, South America, Antarctica, Europe, and Australia. On these continents there are hundreds of different countries.

SOUTH POLE↘

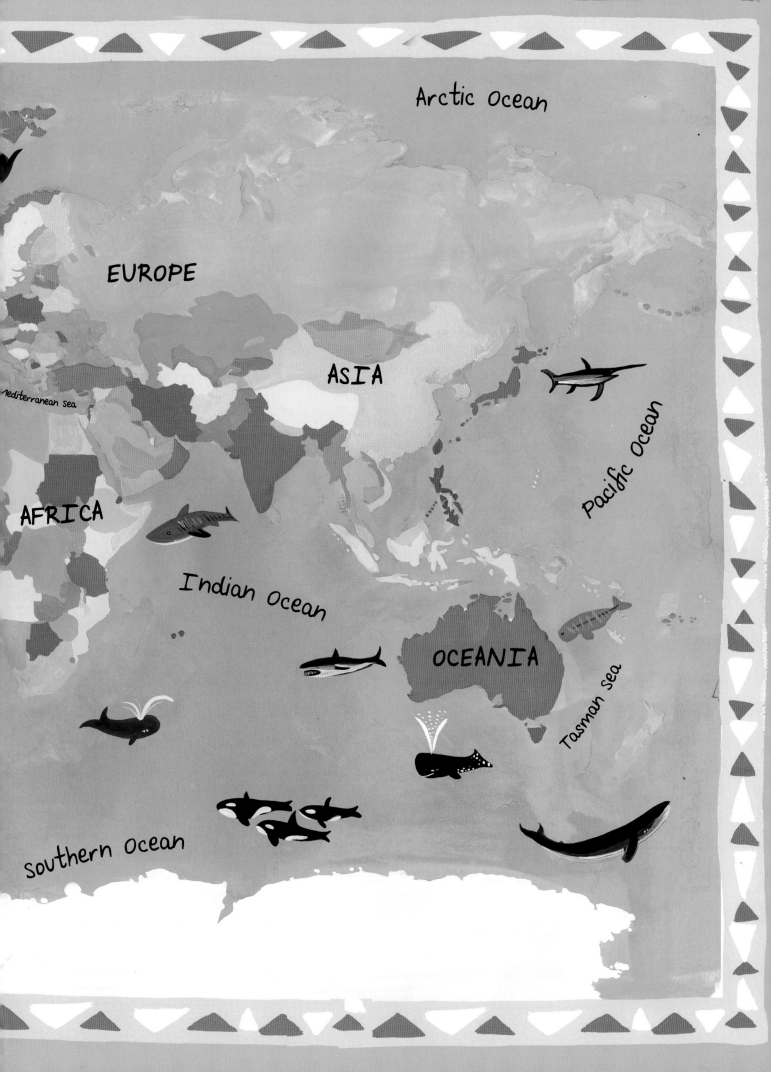

Arctic Ocean

EUROPE

Mediterranean sea

ASIA

AFRICA

Pacific Ocean

Indian Ocean

OCEANIA

Tasman Sea

Southern Ocean

Index

Library of Congress Cataloging-in-Publication data is on file with the publisher.

Copyright © 2012 Red Lemon Press Limited
Illustrated by Christopher Corr
Written by Anita Ganeri
First published in the UK by WeldonOwen Publishing
Published in 2015 by Albert Whitman & Company
ISBN 978-0-8075-0443-7

All rights reserved. No part of this book may be reproduced or transmitted in any
form or by any means, electronic or mechanical, including photocopying,
recording, or by any information storage and retrieval system,
without permission in writing from the publisher.

Printed in Hong Kong
10 9 8 7 6 5 4 3 2 1 HH 20 19 18 17 16 15 14

For more information about Albert Whitman & Company,
visit our web site at www.albertwhitman.com.